A Soldier's Story

# TONY DUFFLEBAG

### ... and Other Remembrances of the War in Korea

## Clarence G. Oliver, Jr.

*AuthorHouse*
1663 Liberty Drive, Suite 200
Bloomington, IN 47403
888.519.5121
www.authorhouse.com

*AuthorHouse™*
*1663 Liberty Drive, Suite 200*
*Bloomington, IN 47403*
*www.authorhouse.com*
*Phone: 1-800-839-8640*

*Oliver, Clarence G., Jr., 1929-*
  *Tony Dufflebag . . . and Other Remembrances of*
  *the War in Korea.*
  *Oliver, Clarence G., Jr.*

*First published by AuthorHouse  11/7/2007*

*ISBN: 978-1-4259-3737-5 (sc)*
*ISBN: 978-1-4343-3736-8 (dj)*

*Printed in the United States of America*
*Bloomington, Indiana*

*This book is printed on acid-free paper.*

# Tony Dufflebag
*. . . and Other Remembrances of the War in Korea*

✦

Clarence G. Oliver, Jr.

Also By
Clarence G. Oliver, Jr.


*Ethical Behavior*
*An Administrator's Guide:*
*Ethics and Values in School Administration*


*One from the Least*
*And Disappearing Generation:*
*A Memoir of a Depression-Era Kid*


*Broken Arrow: The First Hundred Years*
(Contributing Writer and Co-Editor)

# —*Contents*—

| | | |
|---|---|---|
| Prologue | The Heritage | 1 |
| One | A Night to Remember | 13 |
| Two | Inch'on and Beyond | 19 |
| Three | Knights, Heroes and Brothers | 44 |
| Four | Fear is Powerful | 76 |
| Five | Out of the Blue | 83 |
| Six | Hot Shower and More | 90 |
| Seven | By Candlelight | 100 |
| Eight | Restful Night in Yongdungp'o | 106 |
| Nine | The Combat Infantryman | 123 |
| Ten | Rescue of Wounded Warrior | 135 |
| Eleven | Death of an Infantryman | 171 |
| Twelve | Lonely Walk | 175 |
| Thirteen | Tony Dufflebag | 186 |
| Fourteen | God Knows | 205 |
| Fifteen | Shot at and Missed | 221 |
| Sixteen | Thoughts of Home | 232 |
| Seventeen | War of Words | 244 |
| Eighteen | Everything Isn't Black and White | 255 |
| Nineteen | Going Home | 265 |
| Twenty | Home at Last | 276 |
| Twenty One | After Korea | 289 |
| Epilogue | | 293 |
| Acknowledgments | | 306 |
| References | | 311 |

# —Such Good Men—

*"I now know why men who have been to war
yearn to reunite. Not to tell stories
or look at old pictures.
Not to laugh or weep on one another's knee.
Comrades gather because they long to be with the men
who once acted at their best, men who suffered and sacrificed,
who were stripped raw,
right down to their humanity.*

*"I did not pick these men.
They were delivered by fate and the U.S. Marine Corps.
But I know them in a way I know no other men.
I have never given anyone such trust.
They were willing to guard something more
precious than my life.
They would have carried my reputation,
the memory of me. It was part of the bargain we all made, the
reason we were so willing
to die for one another.*

*"As long as I have memory, I will think
of them all, every day.
I am sure that when I leave this world, my last thought
will be of my family—and my comrades,
such good men."*

*By Michael Norman
in his book
<u>These Good Men: Friendships Forged from War</u>
Crown Publishers, Inc.
New York
1989*

*—Dedication—*

To all the "Thunderbirds"
of Company C, 180th Infantry Regiment,
and to their wives and families
who bravely waited at home
for their return.

# Reflections on War

*"There's not much I can tell you about this war.
It's like all wars, I guess—
The politicians talk about the glory of it.
The old men talk about the need of it.
And the soldiers, well, they just wanna go home."
—James Lee Barrett, Author*

*Spoken by Movie Character Charlie Anderson
(played by James Stewart)
In the movie, "Shenandoah," 1965*

*Based on a Screenplay by
James Lee Barrett*

*Directed by
Andrew V. McLaglen*

*Universal Pictures Company, Inc.*

*Prologue: The Heritage—*

The act of recalling past experiences is an interesting process, especially if the memories are of a time long ago.

People and events remembered from the time distance of more than a half-century are sometimes part fact and part perception. The people existed and the events occurred. The recollection most likely becomes a blending of reality and a little bit of wishful thinking.

Someone once said that as old soldiers reflect on activities of long ago, in our minds "We fought harder, ran faster and jumped higher than what we really did and were braver than we really were."

The memories recorded in these writings most likely reflect such thoughts.

I was born at the "tail end" of the generation that frequently has been referred to as "The Greatest Generation."

As a 17-year-old high school student, just a few weeks before the end of my senior year in 1947, I enlisted in the military, joining the famed 45th Infantry Division that was being reorganized as a hometown National Guard unit just two years following the end of World War II. I found myself as a private in Company C, 180th Infantry Regiment.

The heritage of a military unit is important. After talking to some of the older soldiers in the company, I learned that this was a unit that traced its beginnings to the Oklahoma Territory and Indian Territory days—to 1890—when the 1st Infantry Regiment of the Oklahoma Volunteer Militia was formed, later to become part of the Oklahoma National Guard.

The unit saw Federal service in 1898-1899 and again with Mexican Border service in 1916, and then as part of the 36th Division in 1917, with Federal service until June 1919. Reorganization occurred during the days following World War I, resulting in the designation of the unit as the 180th Infantry Regiment in October 1921 as part of the 45th Infantry Division.

The 180th Infantry Regiment became legendary, though, during the battles of World War II.

During my study about Company C and the 180th Infantry Regiment, I learned about a huge cluster of battle streamers displayed on the unit's guidon, plus a beautiful blue banner that indicated the company had been awarded a special Presidential Unit Citation.

I soon found that each of us serving in the unit was authorized to wear on his uniform a blue ribbon, with gold metal border, as recognition of the unit's Presidential award.

That was impressive to a young private.

A quick review of the unit's history led me to know that the award was earned through the outstanding per-formances in Italy of those who made up "the Company," especially during the desperate battles on the deadly Anzio beachhead, at Salerno, and near such far-away places as Oliveto, Italy

Among the great heroes of that company was one Lieutenant Ernest Childers, a Creek Indian from Broken Arrow, Oklahoma, who had been awarded the Medal of Honor, this nation's highest award for wartime valor.

At that time, I did not dream that in a few years, our paths would cross and that the hero, Lieutenant Childers, who became Lieutenant Colonel Childers, and I were to become close friends.

Colonel Childers was born in Broken Arrow, Oklahoma on February 1, 1918, as the third of five children. He enlisted in the Oklahoma National Guard in 1937 while attending the Chilocco Indian School in north-central Oklahoma, and trained with Company C, and other 45th Infantry Division units at Fort Sill, Oklahoma, and in maneuvers Louisiana when he division was placed on active duty in 1940 in the days prior to the United States entering World War II.

By the end of the year the world situation had worsened, and the Thunderbirds continued their training and prepared for war.

The Thunderbirds trained at Fort Sill, Oklahoma; Camp Barkeley, Texas; Fort Devens, Massachusetts; Pine Camp, New York, and Camp Pickett, Virginia. On July 10, 1943 the division participated in their first of four amphibious landings, fighting their way across Sicily, Italy, France, and Germany. In all the division served 511 days in combat during World War II.

The 45th Infantry Division served with General George S. Patton's U.S. 7th Army during the Sicilian campaign, and when the fighting was done, the commander had this to say about the division, "Your division is one of the best, if not the best division in the history of American arms."

3

The then young Lieutenant Childers served with his infantry platoon in those battles in Africa, Sicily and participated in the ferocious Anzio landing and subsequent battles in Italy.

On September 22, 1943, in combat operations near Oliveto, Italy, he was injured. Despite a broken instep that forced him to crawl, Second Lieutenant Childers advanced against enemy machinegun nests, killing enemy soldiers, capturing positions and an enemy mortar observer. His bravery and inspirational action led to his being awarded the Medal of Honor.

Here are the words of the citation for that award:

*"For conspicuous gallantry and intrepidity at risk of life above and beyond the call of duty in action on 22 September 1943, at Oliveto, Italy. Although 2d Lt. Childers previously had just suffered a fractured instep he, with 8 enlisted men, advanced up a hill toward enemy machinegun nests. The group advanced to a rock wall overlooking a cornfield and 2d Lt. Childers ordered a base of fire laid across the filed so that he could advance. When he was fired upon by two enemy snipers from a nearby house he killed both of them. He moved behind the machine gun nests and killed all occupants of the nearer one. He continued toward the second one and threw rocks into it. When the two occupants of the nest raised up, he shot 1. The other was killed by 1 of the 8 enlisted men, 2d Lt. Childers continued his advance toward a house farther up the hill, and single handed, captured an enemy mortar observer. The exceptional leadership, initiative, calmness under fire, and conspicuous gallantry displayed by 2d Lt. Childers were an inspiration to his men."[1]*

---

[1] Citation, Childers Medal of Honor. Achieves 45th Infantry Division Museum

His actions were instrumental in helping the Americans win the Battle of Oliveto. His other military awards included the Combat Infantryman Badge, Europe and Africa Campaign Medals, the Purple Heart, the Bronze Star and the Oklahoma Distinguished Service Cross. He retired from the Army in August 1965 as a Lieutenant Colonel.

Ernest Childers died on March 17, 2005. He was Oklahoma's last Medal of Honor winner still living in the state. He was an honored guest during many Presidential Inaugurations and as a Creek Indian, was named Oklahoma's Most Outstanding Indian by the Tulsa Chapter of the Council of American Indians in 1966.

The Ernest Childers Middle School in his hometown Broken Arrow was named in his honor. His funeral-memorial service was held in that school, attended by a capacity audience. A statue to honor Childers also was commissioned by his hometown leaders. That monumental statue is a centerpiece for Broken Arrow's Veterans Park on that city's Main Street and is the last major statue created by one of the world's greatest sculptors, Allan Houser, who died just days before the unveiling and dedication of the Childers statue in Broken Arrow.

Being a part of a unit where a former member was a Medal of Honor recipient was a tremendous honor. All of us who served in Company C wore that Presidential Unit Citation ribbon with great pride, and tried to uphold the heritage of that company and those brave men who served in the unit in the years before and during the Korean War.

This was a unit with a valiant history. I soon was aware that I was now among and serving with some quiet heroes who had fought in World War II—that conflict that ravaged much of the world during the half-decade of the 1940's.

Those soldiers of the World War II years were joined with those of my age to serve in Armies of Occupation in Japan and Germany, and then were called to fight again in the War in Korea—the so-called "Forgotten War."

Most of the veterans of the Korean War are from the age group generally referred to as the "Depression-era kids." The generation, also the smallest generation in the recent history of this great nation, has been described in various ways, but one depiction, "the Silent Generation," says much about the special traits of this small cohort group.

Some have represented this unique generation as being people who simply have gone about life taking care of business.

That describes those who became the Korean War veterans.

These are the soldiers who unselfishly left their homes to fight in a war that was the first real effort to stop the spread of Communism—ended that war, came home to a people who for the most part ignored them as they had ignored the war, said little about their heroic actions, seldom complained, and returned to a life of work, families and community service.

There were no welcome-home parades or celebrations. The Korean War veterans were soldiers who just came home and continued with our lives.

World War II, the "great war," was barely over before the conflict in Korea erupted. As the result, the Korean War is over-shadowed by World War II.

The Korean War was a bitter war that was fought in a cold and hostile land. The war began on June 25, 1950, when the North Korean Army launched an invasion into South Korea. Before a controversial armistice ground the war to an awkward halt on July 27, 1953, soldiers from the United States and 21 other United Nations countries battled the North Korean and Chinese armies up and down the Korean peninsula for three bloody years.

More than a half-century has passed since that winter day in 1951 when I landed at Inch'on, South Korea, and then moved with my infantry unit into combat positions in the mountains of North Korea, relieving elements of the famed 1st Cavalry Division that were holding the mountains, hills and valleys south and east of the Yokkuk-ch'on River valley and west of Ch'orwan, North Korea.

Military records refer to the time period as the Second Korean Winter. As 1951 drew to a close, the fighting had changed from large scale battles involving massive forces to a war that consisted of artillery duels, ambushes, raids, patrol clashes and bitter small-unit struggles for strategic hills and key outpost positions.

Major offensive operations were halted because key leaders felt the cost of such assaults on the enemy's defensive positions would be very high and the results could not justify great losses of men in those battles.

In addition, there was the possibility than an armistice agreement would be reached as the result of talks between the battling nations.


With the shift in operations from major offensive movements to a concept of active defense, the front line positions began to take on a different look of trenches, fortified bunkers and outposts.

During the 45th Infantry Division's 429 days of combat in Korea, 378 were spent on the Jamestown Line along the Ch'orwon Valley. Those of us who served in the Thunderbird Division became familiar with places with names like T-Bone Hill, Hill 223, Outpost Eerie, Hill 200, Alligator Jaws, Pork Chop Hill, Old Baldy, Heartbreak Ridge and strange sounding names of dozens of small villages in North Korea that rarely appear on maps other than the more detailed military maps used in combat operations.

The 45$^{th}$ Division held the ground against the Communist forces until the peace accord was signed in July 1953. During the period from December 1951 to June 1952, the Division's 179th and 180th Infantry Regiments fought repeatedly over hills and valleys that then seemed strategically important, including Pork Chop Hill, a key piece of terrain that commanded the area.

Even in later months after the 45th Division was relocated to the Eastern side of the Korean peninsula, possession of Pork Chop was still hotly contested.

The so-called "Forgotten War" was not forgotten by the Soldiers, Marines, Sailors, and Airmen who were there—or by their families.


After three years of combat, total casualties of all United Nations forces in Korea reached more than 550,000, including 95,000 dead. American losses included 33,686 killed and 103,284 wounded. The United States Army casualties alone totaled 27,728 dead and 77,596 wounded. The estimate of enemy casualties, including prisoners, exceeded 1,500,000 of whom 900,000 were Chinese.

Those thousands of casualties cannot be "forgotten."

The freedom and prosperity now enjoyed by those who are privileged to live in the United States have been assured, in part, by selflessness and sacrifices of those who fought and died in wars throughout our nation's history.

During the 230-plus years of this nation's remarkable history, millions of Americans have served in almost 15 wars since the Revolutionary War that was fought to begin this nation.

Living in our nation are approximately 25 million veterans of World War I, World War II, the Korean War, the Vietnam War, the more recent Persian Gulf War, the short-term peace-keeping roles in some third world nations such as Grenada, Somalia, Bosnia, the challenging and strange wars in Afghanistan and Iraq—as well as those who have served in peacetime years.

Like other things of great value, this nation and the freedoms we enjoy did not come cheaply.

People need to be aware of that history. Those of us who are a bit more mature are fiercely patriotic, holding deep feelings that were instilled into our minds and hearts during the school years of the 1930's, the 1940's and early 1950's.

Most of us feel a need to pass on those memories, feelings and the associated history.

Many writers have recorded the history of the Korean War, the battles—large and small—and other tales of the horrors of war in a ravaged land. The "tales" told in this book are not so much about combat but are reflections about people, incidents, and feelings—the impressions during a time of war in a far off land.

The memories are shared to gratefully honor all those who have faithfully served this nation.

*Private Clarence G. Oliver, Jr., joined Company C as a 17-year-old high school senior in May 1947. At left, in training a Fort Sill, Oklahoma. (August 1947)*

*Young soldiers in a proud unit—Sergeant Ben C. Floyd and Private First Class William D. Marshall (above) in a "Jeep" at Fort Sill, Oklahoma.*

*Sergeant Clarence Oliver, Jr. (left) and Sergeant Ben C. Floyd pose with Company C guidon at Fort Sill. (August 1948)*

*Lieutenant Ernest Childers, a Creek Indian from Company C, 180ᵗʰ Infantry Regiment, is awarded the Medal of Honor by General Jacob L. Devers in Italy on July 13, 1944.*

*(U.S. Army Signal Corps photograph)*

*An American Hero— Lieutenant Colonel Ernest Childers*

*(1918-2005)*

*(Photo courtesy of HomeOfHeroes.com)*

180<sup>th</sup> Infantry Regiment Crest

Motto
"Tanap Nanaiyakia Altaiyaha"
(Cherokee Language)

"Ready in Peace or War"

# Chapter One

## A Night to Remember—

Even in the hours approaching midnight, the distant outline of the Chinese-held Whitehorse mountain and other battled-scarred mountains were visible across the snow-covered valley west of the war-ravaged city of Ch'orwon, North Korea, as my childhood friend and now fellow soldier Sergeant First Class Stanley D. Walker and I looked from the observation post just forward of the crest of the hill on which Company C soldiers were deployed.

The reported temperature, passed on to us through informal messages over the field telephone that was used to communicate from the forward observation post to the company command post and the 81 mm mortar squads behind the hill, was in the range of 10 degrees below zero, or some such level.

Whether simply at freezing level, zero or even lower, for an Infantryman on the front lines, in a trench or partially open bunker, it was cold.

At some point, a few degrees one way or the other doesn't seem to matter. Freezing is freezing, and Sergeant

Walker and I felt chilled to the bone, despite the thickness of the hooded parkas and winter uniforms both of us wore.

This was a night for reminiscing—New Year's Eve, 1951. People around the world would gather for parties, the singing of "Auld Lang Syne," and to participate in noisy celebrations to welcome the start of a New Year. Although not condoned by any official orders, a different type "noisy" celebration was being planned all along the front lines in Korea.

Surely the North Korean and Chinese soldiers who were hunkered down in trenches, caves and bunkers in the valley before us and in the hills and mountains beyond the valley knew that the Americans most likely would celebrate at midnight by firing virtually every type weapon in the arsenal. The soldiers across the way must have been terrified just thinking about what might happen this night.

Stanley Walker and I had grown up in the same neighborhood in Ada, Oklahoma, attended the same schools, had common friends, belonged to and attended the same church—Oak Avenue Baptist Church where his father was a deacon. His parents were next-door neighbors of my wife's family on West Fourth Street.

Our location this night was miles north of the now-famous 38th Parallel, the one-time dividing line between North and South Koreas, and the place where this war had begun 18 months earlier on Sunday, June 25, 1950, when the North Korea Peoples Army swept across the parallel in a pre-dawn attack, marking the beginning of an open conflict between peoples of a divided country and, in a larger sense, causing the cold war to erupt in open hostilities.

Now, we two Oklahomans—along with thousands of other soldiers from the United States and more than a dozen other countries banded together in the United Nations—were involved in this expanded Korean civil war.

Huddled inside the observation post (OP) bunker that was half-cave, reinforced with partial walls and a thick

14

roof formed by musty, dirt-filled burlap sacks, we two long-time friends talked about days of childhood, growing up, the unexpected war now being fought, and about plans for the future.

This mountain, as well as those across the valley and beyond, and those located east and west, including such names as Old Baldy, Pork Chop Hill, T-Bone Hill, Bloody Ridge, Heartbreak Ridge and dozens of "no-name" hills that had been fought for, won, lost, won again, and some would again become future military objectives yet to be won and lost in days yet to come.

For this night, though, the hill where the observation post was located and part of the Yokkuk-ch'on River valley below belonged to Company C, 180th Infantry Regiment, a unit with a proud history from a previous war and now manned by 200-plus men who were determined that the valor demonstrated by those who fought with the unit through the days of combat during World War II would be matched in this new war that was being fought up and down an Asian peninsula that most of us knew little about until just a year earlier.

"We are fighting in the wrong war, in the wrong place, the wrong time, and we will never become heroes or win many medals," my friend Stanley Walker lamented. He spoke of being in an "unknown land" in an Army fighting "unknown battles" on "unknown hills" and bemoaned the prospect that none of us would have outstanding military careers that were made possible because of heroic action in significant battles—such as some of those fought during World War II.

In some respects, he was right.

Nevertheless, I was among those who felt that this was a war that needed to be fought. I believed that the invasion of the North Koreans, and later the intervention of the Chinese Army into the conflict, was the first effort of

Communist nations to use military force to wrap the tentacles of Communism around people who were "free."

I, too, was right.

But, Stanley Walker was correct with his prophecy that neither of us would become great military heroes in this war.

At the stroke of midnight, though, our nostalgic conversation ended. The night sky suddenly was illuminated by flares fired from the 81mm mortars squads of our own company as well as from supporting artillery units. Then, the ground in the valley before us and the hills and mountains across the valley shuddered as tons of heavy artillery rounds fired from the 105mm and the 155mm howitzers batteries located far behind us rained down again and again and again. The roar of explosions was deafening.

Just as suddenly, after what seemed to be four or five minutes of powerful explosions on the ground and in the sky, the firing ceased.

Those of us who had witnessed this barrage from the observations points, trenches and bunkers along the front lines in North Korea were in awe of the massive display of firepower.

How could anyone serving in the enemy Army across the way survive such a terrible pounding?

All was quiet—for the moment.


In war, the turning of a calendar page to mark the beginning of a New Year doesn't seem to matter very much. The enemy did survive the celebratory New Year's Eve demonstration of firepower. The next day, incoming rounds from the giant and very accurate Chinese 120mm mortars gave evidence that the enemy across the way was very much alive and very capable of waging war.

The New Year—1952—had arrived.

*Whitehorse Mountain area and No Man's land in the Yokkuk-ch'on River valley. Chinese army units occupied the area across the valley.*

*(December 1951)*

*Assistance in building bunkers, carrying water and supplies— and sometimes accompanying combat patrols to serve as litter bearers for wounded—was provided by South Korean civilians in the Korean Service Corps. John McKenna (left) and a Korean worker dig an emplacement.*

# Chapter Two

## Inch'on and Beyond—

Our arrival in Korea was through the Inch'on harbor, that same place where just 14 months earlier, in September 1950, a daring amphibious landing by forces of the 1$^{st}$ Marine Division had stunned the enemy. The landings were a huge success. The U. S. forces severed enemy supply and communication lines, led to the recapture of Seoul, and cut off the North Korean army units that were in South Korea.

Inch'on is a harbor city on the west coast of Korea, a seaport noted for its very narrow harbor, the rocks and shoals, and for its unusual high and low tidal conditions. The infamous coastal tides are considered to be among the most dangerous in the world.

During low tide, the harbor area turns to giant mud flats. Just a few miles inland to the northeast is the South Korea capitol city of Seoul and its suburban industrial-warehouse city, Yongdungp'o, sitting on the Han River that runs northwest to spill into Kanghwa Bay and the Yellow Sea.

There was good reason to call that body of water the "Yellow Sea." The water was colored from the mud and slush coming down out of China and Korea through the mighty Yangtze, Han and other rivers that drained those Asian countries.

Once again, the renowned 45th Infantry Division was to be engaged in combat—this time in Korea. The arrival at Inch'on was the first step on a long journey.

During the previous six months, the 45th Infantry Division had been deployed on the island of Hokkaido with a mission to occupy and defend this northernmost island of Japan and to continue combat training. That Army of Occupation duty was disrupted when orders were received to deploy to Korea.

The intense training during the months of service on Hokkaido proved to be excellent preparation for duty in Korea.

Hokkaido was the second largest and most sparsely populated of the major islands of Japan. The island was once called Yezo, but the name was changed to Hokkaido (the region of the northern sea) in 1869. The island was an excellent military training area because of its rugged interior, heavy vegetation and its many volcanic peaks—one rising to 7,511 feet. And, being the most northernmost island of Japan, Hokkaido also was certainly its coldest. We soon found that the weather in the mountains of North Korea was even colder.

Like all of Japan, the island was subject to earthquakes. Two or three minor earthquakes rattled our camp area during the months the 45th Division trained in Japan.

The northern tip of Hokkaido island was only a few miles from Sakhalin Island, a large Russian island, and from the Kuril Islands, also Russian. During the 180th Infantry's tactical training in the northern portion of Hokkaido, our soldiers could see the Russian islands across the narrow Soya strait and sea-lanes, and even watched Russian paratroopers in their training jumps on the island.

Because of its unique strategic location to the Asian mainland, Hokkaido was a key center of electronic surveillance for gathering intelligence on Russian activities.

The majority of the electronic listening posts and radar centers on Hokkaido were under the control and managed by the Air Force that, in addition to the task of monitoring Russian broadcasts, also tracked movement of all Russian aircraft.


All of us in the unit were very much aware that there was a "hot, shooting war" going on in nearby Korea and a "cold war" playing out in other parts of the world. We knew that our mission in Japan was important, and that danger was ever-present.

Training was constant and intense.

Company C and other units of the 180th Infantry continued to master infantry tactics in the rugged island terrain, engaged in an extensive period of combined arms training, and participated in mock warfare maneuvers throughout the island—daytime and nighttime.

These activities were followed by exercises in preparation for amphibious landings, training with U. S. Marines and the U. S. Navy in combat loading onto landing crafts, loading onto troop ships and performing mock ship-to-shore landings on the coast of Hokkaido.

The level of training intensified as winter months approached and nearby mountains were becoming snow-covered. Several noncommissioned officers in the unit were chosen to receive ski training in preparation for serving as instructors for the remainder of the unit when cross-country ski skills and tactics were to be learned.

Most of us in Company C, especially the Oklahomans, had never skied and the planned for ski training for the entire unit was eagerly awaited. That desired training was not achieved. The Army had more pressing duty in mind for the "Thunderbirds."

The troops in Korea were now under the command of a trusted military leader, General Matthew B. Ridgway.

General Ridgway, the commander of the 82nd Airborne Division in World War II, was a tough, flamboyant, no-nonsense commander who was extremely popular with GI's. General Ridgway had succeeded General Douglas MacArthur as supreme commander in April 1951.

The "firing" of General MacArthur by President Harry Truman received missed reaction among soldiers.

I, for one, was glad.

Those of us in the 45th Infantry Division learned of that command change while our unit was still at sea, headed to the Far East theatre. The change seemingly was applauded by most of the soldiers aboard the *U.S.S. Williams S. Weigel*, the massive troop transport ship loaded with a large contingent of the 180th Infantry Regiment.

Our announced destination was for duty in the Army of Occupation in Japan, and for additional combat training. Aboard ship, though, there were rumors that our unit was headed directly to Korea, possibly even to be involved in an amphibious landing on the east shore of North Korea, not unlike the surprise landing at Inch'on a few months earlier.

Rumors run rampant among soldiers all the time. Obviously, that particular rumor was false.

Whether such a speculated plan had been in the war games planning isn't known; but, when the 180th Infantry Regiment arrived on Hokkaido, nothing much had been made ready for us. The designated area for the 180th Infantry Regiment was on the outskirts of the town of Chitose, near an airbase that had once been a training site for "Kamikaze" pilot—those Japanese pilots who were trained in World War II to make suicide crashes into Allied ships, and who did so very effectively.

As our units arrived to establish a camp, the designated area was covered with small trees. The first task was to clear the land, lay out company streets, erect the 12-man squad tents, dig some foxholes for any possible but unlikely air strikes that might occur on this northernmost of the Japanese islands, and establish a camp. The company streets were filled with tree stumps.

Despite the "official word" that our unit was on a mission to defend Hokkaido, most of us continued to believe that the assignment to northern Japan was a change in plans after General MacArthur was relieved of command. Otherwise, by the often erroneous reasoning of soldiers, the Army would have had some facilities in place to house a full Infantry division of 12,000 or so men.

Rumors continued to be heard for months about a plan for the 45th Infantry Division to lead an amphibious attack into North Korea.

Speculation is always interesting.


During August 1951, senior commanders of organizations of the division were flown to Korea and matched with commanders of the 1st Cavalry Division units to become acquainted with the terrain, the tactical situation, and characteristics of the enemy.

That was an orientation visit that would have implications for all of us in a few weeks.

Following such a visit, these senior officers most certainly were provided official notice that the 45th Infantry Division soon would be deployed to Korea, but no formal notice reached the men in the units.

Most of us suspected that deployment to Korea was imminent.

Rumors of the deployment were heard everywhere—throughout military units and also in the nearby city of Chitose where shop owners, businessmen, citizens on the street and Japanese girls working in the bars and restaurants all said that the "Thunderbirds" were leaving Hokkaido for Korea.

Airlift training was initiated for many of the units. The 180th Infantry Regiment was based at Camp Chitose, adjacent to the Chitose Air Base, and thus had easy access to the airport where transport planes could land and training could be conducted.

Company C, along with other infantry units, began airlift operations training and developed skills in loading of personnel and equipment into C-130s, the large Air Force troop and cargo carriers.

First Sergeant Harold Gene Evans of Ada, Oklahoma, recalled that he was leading the Company C troops in an airlift training activity at the airport when word came to him that the 45th Infantry Division would "ship out soon" for Korea.

On November 18, 1951, the Division was officially alerted for movement to Korea.

Things started to happen.

During the next few days, much of our clothing, shoes, dress uniforms and other non-combat items were turned in to supply. Personal items were packed and shipped home to the United States.

Combat clothing—wool underwear, field pants to wear over wool pants, pile jackets, pile caps, parkas and shoepacs—were issued. Immunizations were checked, more shots given, records updated. Wills were reviewed and updated. New "Power of Attorney" documents were prepared.

At night, hundreds of letters were written to wives, sweethearts, parents, other relatives and friends to share thoughts about what might lie ahead for each of us.


A few days before the scheduled departure, the island of Hokkaido was covered with a heavy snow. Almost overnight, the snow was knee-deep, with drifts up to several feet deep. This deep snow was a harbinger of what might lie ahead for us in Korea—severe cold weather and a great deal of snow.

This was the Thanksgiving season, normally a special holiday for Americans.


Two days after Thanksgiving Day and less than two weeks after the division was alerted for deployment to Korea, Company C and other units in the 180th Infantry Regimental Combat Team (RCT) loaded onto troop ships, climbing aboard with full combat gear—each of us wearing steel helmet, parka, combat pack, cargo pack attached below, horseshoe roll across the top with pup tent, sleeping bag, blanket, and with rifles slung across our shoulder.

The 45th Infantry Division was to be the first National Guard division to deploy in the Korean War. The 180th Infantry Regimental Combat Team (RCT) was the first of the "Thunderbirds" to join in the battle. Other elements of the division would arrive later. By the end of December, the entire division was in Korea.


Soldiers of Company C, along with other units of the First Battalion, 180th Infantry Regiment, climbed aboard the *USS Henrico (APA 45)* at the Port of Otaru, a small harbor town on the western side of the island of Hokkaido, about 50 or 60 miles west of Camp Chitose.

The *Henrico*, on which our unit was combat loaded, was an attack transport ship that had an impressive battle record in World War II and Korea, having participated in invasion landings including the June 6, 1944, Omaha Bench Assault Force in Normandy, the August 1944, invasion of the Mediterranean southern coast of France, then into Pacific theater action, the invasion of Okinawa, the last operation on the long island road to Japan itself. Early in the Korean War, the *Henrico* landed troops at the decisive Inch'on beachhead on September 15, 1950, one of the most brilliantly executed amphibious operations in history.

Sailors on board the ship were proud of the ship and its combat record.

Captain H. W. Taylor, USN, was commanding officer of the *Henrico*, having assumed command of the ship on July 29, 1951. The veteran attack transport had been in the Seattle, Washington, port since late March for repairs. In October, the renovated *Henrico* sailed again for Korea, this time transporting the 14th Marine Replacement Unit, landing the Marines and their equipment on November 4, 1951, at Sok-Cho-Rhi, Korean, 15 miles behind the United Nations lines.

Then, Captain Taylor sailed his ship to Hokkaido, Japan, to begin transporting the 45th Infantry Division from Japan to Inch'on, South Korea, starting with the First Battalion, 180th Infantry Regiment. The ship remained at Inch'on to begin transporting elements of the 1st Cavalry Division to Hokkaido, to assume the defense positions previously held by the "Thunderbirds."

Our trip to Inch'on required approximately five days. While on board the ship, I learned that the *Henrico* was originally named the *Sea Darter* when it was first launched at Pascagoula, Mississippi, shipyards in early 1943. Later in the year, the ship was converted to an attack transport design and was commissioned the *USS Henrico* on November 26, 1943, renamed for historic Henrico County, Virginia.

The *Henrico* was not a huge ship. It measured 75 feet at the beam and was 492 feet in length. The ship carried 15 or so landing craft to be used to transport soldiers from ship to shore in amphibious landings.

The ship could accommodate about 1,200 soldiers in troop quarters and 65 officers in more spacious officers' quarters. The First Battalion, 180th Infantry Regiment, required most of those spaces.


Captain Taylor commanded a very efficient ship with a proud and dedicated crew. The officers and crew made the soldier-passengers feel very welcome on board the ship. The ship, although already a battle-scarred vessel, was well maintained, clean, and efficiently operated by a qualified and experienced crew.

Many of us were surprised when one of the crewmembers showed up in our crowded troop quarters looking for "guys from Company C" who were from his hometown—Ada, Oklahoma. The seaman was a high school classmate of several of the Ada contingent. I have tried my best to recall his first name but simply cannot remember the name other than his last name was Smith. He had chosen to enlist in the U. S. Navy rather than the National Guard when he finished high school.

The reunion was enjoyable. Stories of the hometown, of high school days, of military experiences and other tales were eagerly shared during the few hours all of us were able to spend together before those of us headed into combat started off on a new journey with an uncertain future.

The crew of the *Henrico* knew they were headed back to Japan. The rest of us were headed to the front lines in Korea.

During the hectic days of preparing to leave Japan, I had not been able to purchase a gift that I could mail to my wife, Vinita, in time for Christmas. The ship's store on board the *Henrico* was not well stocked with gift items. One of the sailors heard me discussing the gift need and advised me that he had purchased some nice handmade items when the ship had made a recent brief stop in Hong Kong.

I asked to look at the items and found he had a beautiful and delicately made linen tablecloth with matching dinner napkins. The craftsmanship of the embroidery was superb. After some discussion, I was able to purchase the items from the sailor—at a price very satisfactory to both of us—and I packaged the linen dinner tablecloth set and mailed it in the ship's post office with the hope that it would be delivered to my wife by Christmas.

The U. S. Navy and the United States Post Office delivered the package to the rightful place and right on time.

The linen tablecloth and napkins remain family keepsakes, with many memories attached. For the better part of six decades, the linen items have been regularly pulled forth and proudly placed on the dining table for special holiday occasions.

Each such use usually prompts the re-telling of my hunt for a Christmas gift for my wife, my on-ship purchase from a sailor and memories of that brief time on board a ship named *Henrico*.

Now, after months of preparation for combat, that experience was about to be ours.

The *Henrico* dropped anchor about two or three miles from the Inch'on harbor area on a cold, gray late-November day just before darkness closed in on the harbor. The approaching darkness, gray skies and winter shadows created a cheerless and somewhat dispiriting atmosphere.

The mainland and the harbor city of Inch'on were barely visible across the water. This was to be a nighttime landing—one that added a bit of apprehension to the feelings of all of us who were about to climb into a landing craft and head to the shore. None of us was quite sure about the future and the dangers that most certainly were ahead.

The extreme tides at Inch'on create unusual problems associated with landing troops on the mainland. The ship's draft was too deep to permit direct access to the dock area because of the tides and the vast mud flats that extended into the Yellow Sea. Landing of troops had to be timed from about two hours before high tide through about two hours after high tide.

The troop ship stood offshore as smaller amphibious landing craft were used to off-load the troops and equipment and transport them through the shallow water from ship to shore.

Rather than use the smaller LCVP (Landing Craft Vehicle Personnel) boats on board the *Henrico*, the Army and Navy officers coordinating the landing chose to use larger Landing Ship Utility (LSU) vessels that could transport larger numbers of soldiers on each trip from ship to shore.

Since the LSU was a larger vessel and could pull along side the troop ship, we Infantrymen did not have to crawl over the side by cargo nets, as would have been the case with the smaller LCVP boats. That was a blessing. The cargo net loading had been practiced. This was to be an easier landing.

A narrow ramp was lowered at the side of the ship, and, as darkness fell, Company C's troopers formed a line and unloaded in single file to step into the LSU's open deck, standing shoulder-to-shoulder and row upon row as the landing craft bobbed up and down in the changing tide.

Using the larger landing craft permitted about 500 soldiers, about two rifle companies in strength, to load at one time. The LSU was a modification of the former World War II LCT (Landing Craft Tank) and could transport troops, tanks or cargo from ship to shore. As many as five tanks could be loaded onto an LSU.

For this trip, though, the ship was filled with soldiers, all standing and packed like sardines in a can.

The ship had a shallow draft and thus could maneuver in the shallow harbor. The LSU was 135 feet in length, had a beam of 30 feet, and when fully loaded had a draft of only six or seven feet. At the front was a ramp that could be dropped to the beach so soldiers could land. The front draft was only 36-inches, so the ramp could be dropped on the beach at the water's edge.

Had the smaller LCVP boats been used, as was the case for the original Inch'on landing, loading of troops would have been over the side of the troop ship and into the landing craft using rope cargo nets. Only 36 soldiers can be carried in the 36-ft. long LCVP and the two or three-mile trip to shore is a rough ride, usually resulting in a large number of seasick soldiers before they "hit the beach."

I, for one, was thankful for the LSU ride to the shore.


Running through my mind while loading onto the LSU were thoughts about soldiers who had participated in the daring and war-changing Inch'on landing just a few months earlier. The LSU on which Company C and others were being loaded would move to the shore and dock. No artillery shells or machineguns would be fired at us as our craft approached the shore.

What was it like for those Marines and soldiers who made that daring landing? What were they thinking? How many of them died in that landing?

Those were among the questions I wondered about on the way through Inch'on harbor.

The soldiers who made that invasion came ashore in small landing craft—the LCVP. They were seasick, scared and under small arms and artillery fire during the landings.

Our unit had trained for such landings, and had made several practice landings on the shores of Hokkaido Island in northern Japan. Climbing over the side of a troop ship, and then down a rope cargo net into a landing craft is tricky business, especially when encumbered with rifle, combat pack and the attached cargo pack containing all a soldier's possessions.

Although our unit's landing at Inch'on was less dramatic and without the danger of incoming fire from an enemy on shore, our minds—probably a lot like the soldiers who went before us—were focused on an unknown future in a cold, hostile land.

The dock at Inch'on was blanketed in darkness as Company C's troops left the landing craft and for the first time set foot in Korea.

"A single street light" was the only light on the dock, First Sergeant Gene Evans recalled. He led the company of soldiers in single file "for a mile or so to a waiting train."

The train's so-called passenger cars were unlighted and parked on a rail siding, waiting for us. First Sergeant Evans described the situation with these words:

"It was very dark as we entered the rail cars and felt for a place to sit," he remembered. "The interior of the car was fitted with three shelves running the length of the car."

There weren't any passenger seats—only the shelves on which the soldiers could lie down for nighttime train rids.

"All of us crawled onto the shelves and tried to sleep," First Sergeant Evans explained.


The train moved very slowly through the Korean night.

Sleep was almost impossible. The rail cars were unheated. Cold penetrated our bodies.

First Sergeant Evans remembered that cold train ride with these words:

"I was so cold that my body was shaking. So, I got off the slow-moving train, held onto a rod by the steps and ran along beside the train until I got warm from running. I'm sure glad I didn't lose my hold on the rod."[2]

It was a long night.


The train rumbled through the night to the railroad junction near Uijongbu, a city that had been an agricultural textile and food-processing center before the industrial area was virtually destroyed during the previous months of war. The city, about 25 miles north of Seoul, was an important rail center and becoming a vital military installation for the United Nations forces. Rebuilding was occurring.

Our troop train arrived at Uijongbu just about dawn.

There was expectation among our ranks that General Ridgway would be present to witness the arrival of the lead element of the first National Guard division to enter the

[2] Evans, Harold Gene. Personal Correspondence to author, 2006

fight in Korea. He had visited the division a few weeks earlier during training activities in Japan, presumably to plan with division leaders the deployment of the division to Korea.

Some soldiers said they saw him standing with a group of officers as Company C's troops stepped out of the cramped railroad cars—a smiling General Ridgway, with the two trademark hand grenades attached to his combat pack straps.

I did not see him, but excitement was generated by the comments—true or not—that the man who had been named the supreme commander of all forces in Korea and the United States Far East Command was there to welcome us to Korea.

The 180th Infantry Regimental Combat Team (RCT) was the leading element of the first National Guard division to arrive in Korea.

History was being made. Morale was high.

*The U.S.S. General William Weigel was the "home at sea" for troops of the 180ᵗʰ Infantry Regiment for 32 days in March and April 1951 on a long sea voyage from New Orleans, Louisiana, through the Panama Canal, a stop at San Francisco, California, to load additional troops and then on to the Port of Muroran on the Japanese island of Hokkaido. The massive troop ship, measuring 622 feet in length and with a beam of 74 feet, had a troop capacity of 5,209 soldiers. Folddown canvas bunks were stacked six deep and suspended by chains in large troop cabins.*

*While on board the ship headed to the Far East theatre, soldiers learned that General Douglas MacArthur, the supreme commander of all forces in Korea and the United States Far East Command, had been relieved of command and replaced by General Matthew B. Ridgway. The "firing" of General MacArthur by President Harry Truman received missed reaction among soldiers.*

*Soldiers are packed into close quarters in a troopship. Private First Class Joseph A. Tonrbene of New Orleans, Louisiana, kept his humor.*

*The USS Henrico (APA 45) transported the First Battalion, 180th Infantry Regiment, from Hokkaido, Japan, to Inch'on, Korea, in late November 1951. During the Korean War, the Henrico was awarded the Navy Unit Commendation and nine battle stars.*

*Soldiers were packed into the Landing Ship Utility (LSU) vessel, standing erect in lines and rows, almost like sardines in a can, for the trip from the USS Henrico to Inch'on beach and dock area.*

*The smaller Landing Craft Vehicle Personnel (LCVP) boats (below) were similar to those used in the famous September 1950 Inch'on landing. The 45th Infantry Division troops trained for similar amphibious landings before leaving for Korea.*

The greatly respected 180th Infantry Regiment was now "on the ground" in Korea, soon to be followed by the remainder of the 45th Infantry Division, the first National Guard division to be sent into combat in the Korean War.

Most of us had deep personal feelings about our reasons for fighting this war in a land so far from home. But General Ridgway stated the reasons rather eloquently in a memorandum he sent to commanders and troops. I liked the message he sent.

He wrote:

*"The real issues are whether the power of Western civilization, as God has permitted it to flower in our beloved lands, shall defy and defeat Communism; whether the rule of men who shoot their prisoners, enslave their citizens, and deride the dignity of man, shall displace the rule of those to whom the individual and his individual rights are sacred; whether we are to survive with God's hand to guide and lead us, or to perish in the dead existence of a Godless world.*

*"If these be true, and to me they are, beyond any possibility of challenge, then this has long ceased to be a fight for our Korean Allies alone and for their national survival. It has become, and it continues to be, a fight for our own freedom, for our own survival, in an honorable, independent national existence."*[3]

I was proud to be a small part of a military command led by General Ridgway. During our weeks of additional combat training in Japan, the news of the fighting in Korea was followed closely.

We knew the story of how General Ridgway had taken charge of a dispirited army and rebuilt it in a few short months, leading it into battle against the Chinese and

---

[3] Ridgway, (Memorandum, January 21, 1951).

North Korean forces, forcing them back over the 38th parallel.

Now, those of us in the Thunderbird Division were moving into North Korea, ready to continue the fight against Communist forces.

A bittersweet "victory" would come in time.


After the nighttime "sleeper" train ride from Inch'on to Uijongbu, the sleepy, stiff and aching soldiers climbed off the train and assembled in company formation to prepare for the next leg of our journey to the front lines. A quick breakfast was consumed and our company loaded onto trucks and Jeeps and our convoy moved north toward a staging area a few miles behind the front lines.

The next day our unit moved on foot into an area behind the positions that were being occupied by the 1st Cavalry Division. Orders were given to "dig in" and wait for nightfall in preparations for a midnight replacement of troops of the 5th Cavalry Regiment of the 1st Cavalry Division.

"Digging in" was an order that suggested that the small entrenching tool each of us carried on the outside of our combat pack would be used to dig a "foxhole" in the ground to serve as a place of safety in the event that incoming enemy artillery fire might fall on the area.

The temperature was well below zero degrees. The ground was frozen solid. There wasn't much "digging" taking place. Each of us chipped away at the frozen dirt in an effort to create even a small indention into the rock-like ground. Each foxhole was only a few inches deep.

Darkness fell. After awhile, most of us stopped the attempt to dig deeper and simply pulled our parkas tightly around our bodies and with our rifles pulled close we rolled into the shallow indentions and tried to grab a little sleep before beginning the midnight replacement of the 1$^{st}$ Cavalry Division troops.

Everyone was still and silent. There wasn't much sleeping taking place during those hours just before midnight.

To say that most of us were "scared" isn't an accurate description of what was taking place that night. Each of us had an uneasy feeling about what might occur during the night or the next day and the days beyond.

The great adventure of being in combat was about to begin.

I don't know about others, but I spent a great deal of time that night talking with God.

*Moving up! The "bear" in a parka is Master Sergeant Clarence G. Oliver, Jr., on break during an early morning convoy toward new frontline positions. Temperature was reported at 8 degrees below zero.*

*Corporal Donald Peterson, Sergeant First Class Paul Scott and Sergeant John Matthews (below) chow down after trying to warm their frozen C-rations.*

*(December 1951)*

*Temperature for a day or two warmed up to the 20 degrees level in early February 1952 and we thought spring had arrived. That was wrong. Some of us removed tops of our winter clothing, pretended the cold didn't bother us, and played in the snow for a few minutes. Company C was in a reserve position a few miles south of the Main Line of Resistance (MLR).*

*Pictured (front row, left to right) are Sergeant First Class Paul N. Scott, Ada, Oklahoma, and Corporal Donald J. Peterson, Sioux Falls, South Dakota; (back row, left to right) are Corporal Bernard W. Whiting, St. Francis, South Dakota; Corporal Walter H. Flittner, Union City, New Jersey, and Master Sergeant Clarence G. Oliver, Jr, Ada, Oklahoma.*

*Whiting and Peterso, with their South Dakota roots, handled the cold better than some of us "Okies."*

The P-38 Can Opener is considered one of the Army's greatest inventions and was used to open C-ration cans. This P-38 was carried by Clarence Oliver in Korea—and afterwards.

The "US ARMY POCKET CAN OPENER" was commonly known by its nickname," the P-38," which it supposedly acquired from the 38 Punctures required to open a C-Ration can.

Military I.D. "dog tag" worn by Clarence Oliver during the Korean War.

The US Army dog tags recorded the surname, given name, service number, blood type, religion and the date of the soldier's last tetanus shot.
Tags were for identification of dead and wounded.

*Unexpected Christmas gifts from the California Chamber of Commerce, sent to "soldiers in Korea," were distributed to everyone in Company C—and presumably to other units in the 45th Infantry Division. First Lieutenant Howard Nicks (left) hands out the gifts to the assembled troops.*

*No one explained why the Oklahoma units received gifts from California. Some speculated that since the 40th Infantry Division, a California National Guard division also was being deployed to Korea that the California business group was honoring men in both the National Guard units. California Governor Earl Warren visited some 40th Infantry Division units in January 1952.*

# Chapter Three

## Knights, Heroes and Brothers—

*"A hero is no braver than an ordinary man, but he is braver five minutes longer."*
*—Ralph Waldo Emerson*

Heroes do not set out to be such. Most who have become heroes are average people who found themselves in unusual circumstances in which they simply reacted spontaneously—perhaps more quickly that another or for a bit longer than another—and suddenly they had made a difference.

The finest of the brave military men of medieval days often were given a title of "Knight." The title was in recognition of personal merit or service to their country. Some of them were famous as heroes and champions of just causes. Ideally, they formed a "brotherhood" with a commitment to a common cause. During battle, the Knights often entered into face-to-face combat with an enemy.

In more recent wars, the Infantryman became the modern "Knight," the individual who performs that role of being on the "front line" with an enemy always nearby and often "face-to-face."

There are all kinds of heroes, and Company C had many among the mixture of soldiers who had been assembled from all across the nation, brought together and molded into one of the finest military units ever assembled. A most capable team of officers and noncommissioned officers led the unit.

The cadre of noncommissioned officers—the NCOs—was unique. At the core were the men from the hometown National Guard unit who were called to active duty, given the mission of reopening a closed military base, repairing the facilities, receiving and integrating into the unit another 80 or so newly-drafted soldiers, training that unit for combat and then leaving for an overseas assignment within six months.

The mission was accomplished within the limited time schedule.

Many of the NCOs in the company had trained together for several years prior to the beginning of the war in Korea. Some had attended school together since childhood years, played together on athletic teams and participated in other school activities.

They were like family—and, in fact, some were family—brothers, cousins, uncles, nephews and brothers-in-law.

Infantry companies, those unique Army units that go face-to-face with the enemy in battle, depend on NCO leadership perhaps more than most military units. The strong team of NCOs in Company C became extensions of the outstanding officers who led the unit in preparing for and entering combat.

In writing about the Infantry Rifle Company in his extensive study of *Infantry Operations and Weapons Usage in Korea*, General S.L.A. Marshall praised the leadership skills of noncommissioned officers, the valued NCOs, with these words:

> *"Compared to the role of the junior officer, he (the NCO) has come forward much more prominently as a battle leader than during World War II. He exercises more personal initiative than his predecessor and is less disposed to wait for officer approval before taking local decision in an emergency situation. In consequence, there is greater stability and evenness of performance in the combat line."*[4]

The first year of the Korean War was a time of large-scale troop movements and bloody battles in both North and South Korea as the opposing armies swept up and down the length of the Korean peninsula.

That war strategy began to change when the leaders of supporting countries—the United States with its commitment to the South Korean forces and China and Russia in support of the North Koreans—led in an effort to begin negotiations to end the war. Those truce talks would drag on for another two years. The fighting continued.

By the start of the second winter of the Korean War, the strategy of conducting sweeping movements and massive battles over vast areas shifted to one of smaller units attempting to seize or defend key positions along the front that stretched across the entire peninsula.

---

[4] Marshall (1950) p.51

Combat operations often became a series of small raids, patrols, platoon or squad-size attacks—sometimes to probe enemy positions, sometimes to seek to capture enemy prisoners for interrogation purposes, sometimes to establish outposts in the no-man's land in front of the Main Line of Resistance (MLR).

Such small unit tactics were extremely dangerous, required a great deal of courage and often involved personal fighting—man against man.

Almost immediately after the 180th Infantry Regimental Combat Team landed in Korea and before moving into combat positions in the mountains overlooking the Yokkuk-ch'on River valley, west of Ch'orwan, North Korea, several new soldiers were assigned to the unit.

These men only recently had arrived in Korea for assignment to the 1st Cavalry Division and had not yet been in combat. The new soldiers boosted Company C's strength to about 10 to 15 percent above typical authorized level.

This influx of additional men most likely was because someone in a rear-echelon operations section anticipated that casualties soon would reduce the numbers after the unit began combat operations.

After discussion among the unit leaders, a decision was made that the new unit members should be divided among Company C's four platoons, resulting in each squad being increased in size by two or three extra men.

One of those newly assigned soldiers was an experienced noncommissioned officer, Master Sergeant George F. McCorkle, a Regular Army career soldier. His assignment to the unit gave the company commander the luxury of an extra senior noncommissioned officer—and, in this case, one who also even had experience as a commissioned officer.

The commander had two field "first sergeants," Master Sergeant Gene Evans, who held the official title, and Master Sergeant George F. McCorkle.

First Sergeant Evans was one of the hometown leaders who, as did many of us, joined Company C right out of high school, trained hard, studied hard, and assumed leadership roles quickly. Being a leader came easy for him. He was quarterback of the Ada High School Cougar football team during his senior year. His good athletic skills and mental quickness shown on the athletic field transferred to his leading a larger team of soldiers in training and in combat.

His family owned a major Main Street business in Ada, the Evans Hardware Company.

Master Sergeant McCorkle, was a combat infantryman in World War II, and previously held a reserve officer's rank of First Lieutenant. During the reduction of forces following World War II, in order to remain on active duty, he returned to noncommissioned officer status as a Master Sergeant.

McCorkle was from Coatsville, Pennsylvania. He became a close friend.

This was an experienced soldier—both as an officer and as a noncommissioned officer—and, as such, he became a valuable aide to the company commander, to First Sergeant Gene Evans, and to me.

*Captain Lawrence Craig McBroom commanded Company C in the United States and Japan. He became Headquarters Company commander.*

*First Lieutenant Howard J. Nicks commanded Company C in Japan and led the unit into Korea in December 1951.*

*Captain Garnet E. Mercer assumed command in Korea and led Company C during the 1951-1952 winter-spring campaigns.*

49

*First Sergeant Harold Gene Evans (left) of Ada, Oklahoma and Master Sergeant George F. McCorkle of Coatsville, Pennsylvania, were capable senior noncommissioned officers for Company C, 180th Infantry.*

*(January 1952)*

*First Lieutenant Raymond O. Parnell (left) of Wewoka, Oklahoma, Executive Officer, and Second Lieutenant Leland W. Kiker of Childress, Texas. Parnell was a former paratrooper turned Infantry officer. Kiker was a graduate of Texas A&M University and a World War II veteran.*

*(January 1952)*

*First Lieutenant Howard Nicks of Wetumka, Oklahoma, a peacetime newspaper editor, was Executive Officer and served briefly as Company Commander of Company C in Japan as the unit prepared for its initial assignment in Korea. He soon was promoted to Captain and assumed command of another unit.*

*(January 1952)*

Bunkers were our "home away from home." Sergeant John Matthews and First Lieutenant Raymond Parnell check progress on a bunker being built for Executive Officer Parnell.

Below is a snow-covered Company C command post area.

*A dejected-looking Sergeant Robert J. Della Torre of Willimonsett, Massachusetts, a senior medic assigned to Company C from Medical Company, 180th Infantry Regiment, stands at the entrance to Company C Medical Aid Station.*

*Second Lieutenant Frank Fleet of Ada, Oklahoma was a forward observer assigned to Company C from Battery A, 171st Field Artillery Battalion.*

*(January 1952)*

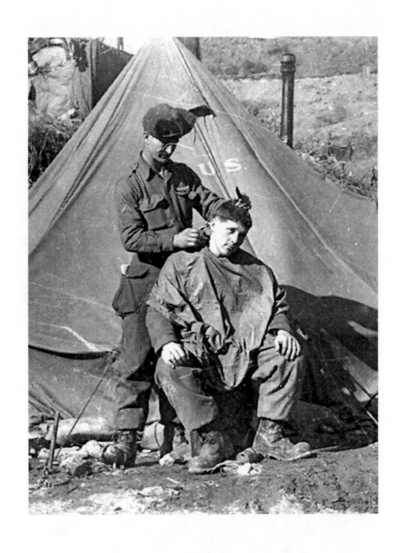

*Corporal Fred L. Jones of Ada, Oklahoma,
turned part-time barber to trim the hair of
Corporal Jack Jones, also of Ada.*

*(March 1952)*

*Kim, a 14-year-old Korean boy educated at a Presbyterian mission school in Pusan, South Korea, is pictured with Master Sergeant George McCorkle (left) and Corporal Donald Peterson. Kim was a major help as an interpreter for Company C, especially with Korean Service Corps men who assisted in carrying supplies and other work. He spoke English, Korean, Chinese and French languages.*

*(January 1952)*

*Mail Clerk Corporal Thomas E. Bardrick (left) of Fort Smith, Arkansas, prepares a money order for Private First Class John W. Ellingboe of Milwaukee, Wisconsin, so he can send funds home to his family.*

*(March 1952)*

*Sergeant Joe Mac Floyd became Company C's first casualty in the snow-covered mountains of North Korea. Evacuation of this wounded soldier was difficult because of the mountainous terrain and the deep snow.*

*A chain of soldiers of the Second Platoon are pictured pulling the severely wounded soldier up a step slope.*

*(AP Wirephoto)*

*December 1951*

# Joe Mac Floyd Is Wounded

**Young Adan with Co. C, 180th Inf., 45th Div. Wounded in Korea Dec. 20**

Corporal Joe Mac Floyd, 19, son of Mr. and Mrs. Furman Floyd, 517 West Ninth, was wounded in action in Korea on December 20.

A telegram reached Ada Saturday informing his parents of that fact, with no additional information.

Cpl. Floyd was with Co. C, 180th Infantry, 45th Division.

He was graduated from Ada highschool in the spring of 1950, and in September of that year went with his outfit to Camp Polk, La., for training and then on to Hokkaido, Japan.

Information was released recently that units of the Thunderbird Division were in Korea and letters had already begun to come in here telling of some of the men being under mortar fire.

*The news of Joe Mac Floyd's injury appeared in the hometown newspaper, "The Ada Evening News," in late December 1951.*

In the Army as elsewhere, spirits soar a bit on "Pay Day." Being "at the front" didn't change that situation. Soldiers want to be paid—even in combat.

Serving as the unit paymaster normally was among my administrative responsibilities, and, as was true of paymasters of each unit along the front, I moved from bunker to bunker across the snow-covered hills on pay day to pass out the Army military pay certificates to all men who wished to be paid.

Some soldiers turned down their pay so that it would accumulate on pay records for later use. Others accepted their money but then made soldiers' deposits.

Many sent money orders to their families. The 45th Division post office unit had made arrangements for men, even in front line positions, to be able to purchase money orders. Corporal Thomas E. Bardrick, Company C's mail clerk whose hometown was Fort Smith, Arkansas, was kept busy handling the money order transactions.

The December pay period brought a surprise to the men. Pay envelopes were a bit "fatter" since the Korean duty made possible some income tax exempt status for combat zone service. Others, though, ended up with smaller amounts after newly authorized allotments to family members were deducted. Many men, especially the married men, made arrangements for allotments to family members before the unit left Japan and retained only enough cash for anticipated incidental items they planned to purchase while in combat.

Keeping only $10 or $15 each month was common. Some soldiers were surprised to find that many items—candy, razor blades, soap and cigarettes—came to them in the form of a PX (Post Exchange) ration allocation.

Acts of heroism happen almost spontaneously. Sometimes the action is acknowledged and awarded. Often, though, there are many acts of valor that go unrecognized.

The Korean War began just five years after the end of World War II and those officers and noncommissioned officers who were likely to recommend someone for a military award were careful—perhaps overly careful—not to recommend awards too quickly.

Many acts of valor and meritorious service deserved recognition that never came.

The first awards for valor in combat for men of the 180th Infantry came in December 1951. For heroic performances only six days after landing in Korea, three men of the 180th Infantry Regiment were awarded Bronze Star medals for valor.

One of the men was a former member of Company C, Lieutenant Richard Bell of Ada, Oklahoma, who left the unit to attend Officers Candidate School and returned to the Regiment for assignment to another company after being commissioned a Second Lieutenant.

The three received the medals for courage demonstrated by entering an enemy mine field to treat four men who had been wounded by land mine explosions. The incident occurred on December 11, 1951. In addition to Lieutenant Bell, Bronze Star medals also were awarded to Master Sergeant Harold V. Hayes of Holdenville, Oklahoma, and Corporal Charles J. Grurinskas of Boston, Massachusetts.

Lieutenant Bell was the commander and Master Sergeant Hayes was the platoon sergeant of the regimental headquarters security platoon. Corporal Grurinskas was a medic from the Regimental Medical Company.

The four wounded soldiers were members of Lieutenant Bell's platoon. When they were injured, the platoon leader, the platoon sergeant and the medic, all with disregard for their own personal safety, entered the minefield area to treat and rescue the wounded soldiers.

The orders awarding the Bronze Star to Lieutenant Bell told the story of his heroism on December 11, 1951, near Taptong-Ni, Korea with these words:

"Members of Lieutenant Bell's unit were moving into a new assembly area when four of his men were felled by an enemy land mine. Lieutenant Bell leaped over a barbed wire barrier and, disregarding personal safety, raced across an active mine field to the stricken soldiers. Quieting them with calm assurance, he then aided in administering first aid.

"Thereafter Lieutenant Bell carefully, but expeditiously, supervised their evacuation, guiding his comrades safely out of the mine field. His actions prevented further danger and discomfort to the wounded and aided materially in increasing morale among his men. The courage, determination and leadership displayed by Lieutenant Bell reflect great credit on himself, the Infantry, and the United States Army."[5]

One of the wounded soldiers died from the injuries received. All four were awarded the Purple Heart.

Lieutenant Bell joined Company C in 1947, at the end of a delayed senior year in high school, when the National Guard unit was being reorganized following World War II. His high school education had been interrupted when he joined the United States Navy in the waning days of World War II. Following the war, he returned to his hometown to complete his high school education, joined the hometown National Guard unit, and was soon promoted to Sergeant.

---

[5] Undated Newspaper Article, Archives, 45th Infantry Division Museum

61

An older brother had been killed while serving in World War II. The United States Congress had adopted a new law that provided that the "sole surviving son" of a family that lost a son in war should be exempt from wartime military service. When the 45th Infantry Division was called into active service at the start of the Korean War, then Sergeant Bell could have been discharged from service as a "sole surviving son."

He chose to remain in the service, left Company C to attend Officers Candidate School, and after being commissioned a Second Lieutenant, Infantry, returned to the division and was assigned as a platoon leader in Headquarters and Headquarters Company, 180th Infantry Regiment. He was serving in that capacity when his act of valor was performed.

Even though he was in another unit, his long-time friends in Company C still "claimed" this hometown soldiers as "one of our own."

Unit loyalty runs deep.


The men of the 45th Infantry Division became all too familiar with strategic hills and areas with names like T-Bone, Hill 223, Outpost Eerie, Hill 200, Alligator Jaws, and Pork Chop Hill.

During the period from December 1951 to June 1952, the Division's 179th and 180th Infantry Regiments fought repeatedly over Pork Chop Hill, a rather small but strategically important bit of terrain. During February and March 1952, Company C and other units of the First Battalion, 180th Infantry Regiment, held positions that overlooked that now-famous hill.

Officially it was designated Hill 255. The hill's contour lines on a military map gave it the appearance of a pork chop—and imaginative soldiers gave it that name.

In later years, after the war, the hill was made famous through a 1959 film starring Gregory Peck that was based on a book by military historian S.L.A. Marshall. The movie dealt only with the two-day battle for Pork Chop Hill in April 1953.

But, the battles for, over and near Pork Chop Hill started long before the one battle told about in the movie. During the three years of the Korean War, that hill claimed the lives of hundreds of soldiers from the United States, Thailand, Colombia, the Republic of Korea (ROK) and, of course, China.

The struggle for that hill lasted longer than on any other single battlefield in Korea.

Company C's infantryman knew of Pork Chop Hill all too well.


Pork Chop Hill was not a tall mountain. It was a good size hill, wide across the northeast end and with a narrow finger extending to the southwest, giving it a shape that truly did resemble a pork chop. The hill was a strategic point for the valley and overlooked a route along which the Chinese soldiers could infiltrate.

Control of Pork Chop Hill became very important— for both armies.

A small unit combat operation that would take a patrol to that area was ordered for elements of Company C in February 1952. Captain Mercer, the unit's commanding officer, chose the second platoon to handle the mission. This was to be reconnaissance patrol along the Chinese Army's main line of resistance (MLR) and a probing attack, seeking to penetrate the Chinese line. The mission was to determine the strength of the Chinese forces in that area.

Attached to the platoon for that combat mission were two medics from the 180th Infantry Medical Company and eight Korean Service Corps (KSC) civilians who were designated as stretcher-bearers. That medical and evacuation support would be needed.

Sergeant First Class Joe Hill Floyd of Ada, Oklahoma, led one of the rifle squads that participated in the combat operation. A half-century later, Sergeant Floyd told of the battle action. The events of that day were recalled with clarity.

His rifle squad was in the lead position in the pre-dawn hours when the platoon left Company C's front line positions and crossed the main line of resistance (MLR) into the valley. With him was Sergeant First Class James A. West, another of the hometown National Guard unit non-commissioned officers who shortly after the unit arrived in Korea had asked for assignment to a rifle platoon after serving previously as the unit's mess sergeant. Captain Mercer honored that request and transferred Sergeant West to the second platoon. He became an assistant platoon sergeant.

Sergeant Floyd remembered that he had his lead squad in a "squad diamond" formation with individuals about 50-yards apart. He was in the center of the "diamond," the proper place for the squad leader. One of the medics and four Korean civilian litter bearers followed as the squad moved over a small hill that was located between two larger hills and then into a second valley on the other side.[6]

"After we got to the smaller hill, we went over it and there was another valley and we penetrated into the second valley for about 1.5 miles," Sergeant Floyd recalled.

The patrol had reached an area near the ruins Changgun-gol village on the western edge of Hill 255—Pork Chop Hill.

Suddenly, the squad leader spotted a freshly abandoned mortar position, with some of the aiming stakes still

---

[6] Floyd, Joe Hill. Personal correspondence to the author, December 9, 2004.

in place. That spelled trouble. Mortar positions are always placed in locations behind the lines. Sergeant Floyd quickly determined that the patrol was "behind the enemy lines."

"I knew that even the Chinese didn't put their mortars on the very front," Sergeant Floyd recalled. "This could only mean that we were being set up for an ambush."

The squad needed to "get out" quickly.

Sergeant Floyd contacted the platoon leader and suggested that the platoon reverse direction. The platoon leader concurred and as the platoon changed direction, Sergeant Floyd's rifle squad was now in the rear of the platoon combat formation.

"The Chinese forces let us get back to the small hill, and let all of the platoon through a gap except for my squad," Floyd recalled.

The squad members had to reduce interspersing distance between men to go over the small hill. When that occurred, the squad began receiving intense small arms fire and mortar fire from the Chinese forces located in positions higher on the larger hills.

Almost immediately, one man fell. Down was the medic—Private First Class Duane M. Laws of Mexico, New York. Shrapnel from an exploding mortar round had wounded him. Seconds later, one of the Korean litter bearers was wounded by small arms fire while the men were dragging the wounded medic to temporary cover of a small mound of dirt.

"We managed to get the wounded litter bearer to a safer area and then we started returning the small arms fire and machinegun fire with our own rifle fire," Sergeant Floyd explained.

The Chinese machinegun fire was coming from a position in a heavily fortified bunker on the nearby hill. Sergeant Floyd began firing at the opening in bunker wall, killing or wounding the Chinese soldiers inside the bunker.

The machinegun fire ended immediately.

Intense small arms fire from "burp guns" the Chinese soldiers were using continued to keep the squad pinned down.

Sergeant Floyd said that as he looked toward where the rest of the platoon had moved before the ambush firing began, he saw Private First Class Arthur M. Walker, the other medic, "running full blast right toward us. He was ignoring bullets."

Private First Class Walker reached the location where the wounded Private First Class Laws lay on the ground and dressed the injured medic's wound while in full sight of the Chinese who were shooting at him with their burp guns. Miraculously, he escaped injury. The two wounded men were pulled to a safer location near a small mound of dirt.

Now, with the entire squad pinned down by intense automatic weapons fire, and with two wounded men to save, the squad was in a perilous situation.

Getting the squad and the wounded men "out" became the top priority for Sergeant Floyd and Sergeant West, the two senior noncommissioned officers leading the second squad.

In the process, both men—and the medic who ran to aid others—would perform courageous acts.

Acts of bravery aren't planned. They happen. Somehow, faced with the need to "do something," people react by instinct or training and perform in an unusual manner—even when scared half to death.

Sergeant First Class Floyd, Sergeant First Class West and Private First Class Walker each performed acts of bravery that day as they rescued the wounded and made possible the safe return of the entire squad.

The second rifle squad, at the moment the platoon reversed direction, became the platoon's rear guard to prevent or delay the enemy in its approach of the platoon in the withdrawal from the encounter with enemy forces.

Now, the small squad needed a "rear guard" of its own as an attempt was made to break away from contact with the Chinese troops, evacuate the two wounded men, and rejoin the rest of the second platoon.

The two NCOs, Sergeants Floyd and West, assumed responsibility to move the two wounded men to a safer area.

Placing the wounded medic over his shoulder in a fireman's carry position, Sergeant West ran toward a safer area with bullets from the Chinese burp guns hitting at his heels. Sergeant Floyd provided covering fire to distract the Chinese soldiers.

The wounded Korean litter bearer was also carried to safety.

With the wounded men in a safer area, the squad members could now start an evacuation. Sergeant West and Sergeant Floyd began providing covering fire to start the evacuation of the squad members. Moving about 30 yards at a time, with others providing covering fire, the squad members began to break away from the enemy using a "leap frog" technique to reach a safer position.

Everyone was safely extracted and the platoon returned to Company C's positions along the MLR—the Main Line of Resistance.


After learning the details of the action from reports of squad members and others who observed from a distance, I drafted for Captain Mercer's consideration the recommendations that Sergeant Floyd and Sergeant West be considered for medals of valor—the Bronze Star—for their acts of bravery and leadership. The officers of the 180th Medical Company prepared a similar document recommending an award of valor for Private First Class Walker,

Months later, those awards were presented to the brave soldiers.

Sergeant First Class Joe Hill Floyd and Sergeant First Class James A. West, both of Ada, Oklahoma, were awarded the Bronze Star with a V for valor after their return home from service in Korea in an impressive ceremony at the hometown National Guard Armory in Ada. Major Lewis Colbert directed the ceremonies and made the presentations.

Private First Class Arthur M. Walker of Toccoa, Georgia, the medic, was awarded the Silver Star.


Many people go to war. Only a small percentage of those in the military find themselves in direct contact with the enemy.

These are the modern-day "Knights."

There is a unique bond among those who have shared such experiences—especially for those who wear the special award of the silver and blue Combat Infantryman Badge.

# Bronze Star
# To Lt. Bell

*News of the heroic action of Lieutenant Richard Bell appeared on the front page of the Ada Evening News.*

*(December 1951)*

The first Bronze Star medal won by a Thunderbird since the 45th Division went into combat in Korea has been awarded Lt. Richard Bell, Ada.

Bell is an Ada highschool graduate. He was a good student and athlete in highschool. He attended East Central State college here, and played tennis on the college squad.

He is the son of Mrs. Vada Bell, 510 South Townsend. Mrs. Bell had a son killed during the last war, Lt. Jack Bell, who was decorated numerous times for his aerial exploits in the South Pacific theater as a fighter pilot.

The orders awarding the Bronze Star to Lt. Richard Bell tell the story of his heroism. He "distinguished himself by heroic achievement on 11th December, 1951, near Taptong-Ni, Korea.

"Members of Lieutenant Bell's unit were moving into a new assembly area when four of his men were felled by an enemy land mine. Lieutenant Bell leaped over a barbed-wire barrier and, disregarding personal safety, raced across an active mine field to the stricken soldiers. Quieting them with calm assurance, he then aided in administering first aid

*Lieutenant Richard Bell of Ada, Oklahoma, was awarded the Bronze Star for Valor. Originally in Company C, he left for Officers Candidate School, was commissioned a Second Lieutenant, and later returned for leadership assignments in the 180th Infantry Regiment.*

69

*Bronze Star medals for Valor were awarded to Sergeant First Class Joe Hill Floyd (above) and Sergeant First Class James A. West (right) for their heroic action on a combat patrol in an area near the ruins of Changgun-gol village on the western edge of Hill 255— Pork Chop Hill.*

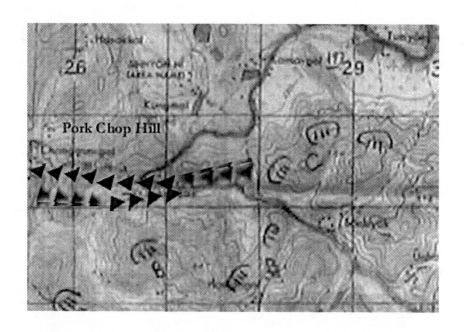

*Company C, 180ᵗʰ Infantry Regiment, occupied front line positions in an area east of Pork Chop Hill in February 1952. The route of the combat patrol and the heroic rear guard fight and evacuation by Sergeant First Class Joe Hill Floyd and Sergeant First Class James A. West and the second platoon from the area near Changgun-gol village is indicated by ◄◄◄◄ symbols.*

*(Military Operations Map, 180ᵗʰ Infantry Regiment, Archives, 45ᵗʰ Infantry Division Museum)*

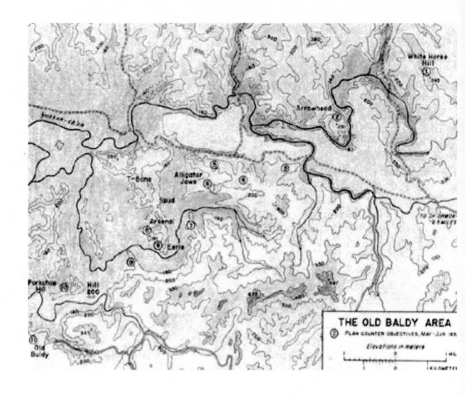

THE OLD BALDY AREA

*In December 1951, the 45ᵗʰ Infantry Division arrived on the Korean peninsula and took up defensive positions in the Yonch'on-Ch'orwon areas in North Korea. The primary mission was to hold their sectors and drive off any enemy advances. All through 1952 the 45th engaged in numerous small battles at Old Baldy, T-Bone Hill, Pork Chop Hill, Outpost Eerie, Alligator Jaws, Heartbreak Ridge and other places along the sectors. In every instance the Thunderbirds held their ground and the North Koreans and Chinese armies never broke through.*

*Buddies from Company C's second platoon enjoy a day in the sun.*
*Pictured (left to right) are) Corporal Kemper W. Chambers.*
*Rockaway, New Jersey, Private First Class Bill Bennett, Washing-*
*ton, D.C., a medic from 180th Medical Company, and Private*
*First Class William (Bill) E. Burke, Neptune, New Jersey.*
                    *(Spring 1952)*

        *(Photo courtesy Kemper W. Chambers)*

*Nothing like a great cigar after lunch! First Lieutenant Warner B. (Hook) Eales of Ada, Oklahoma, takes time to enjoy a good cigar as he sprawls in front of the Company B command post. Lieutenant Eales was a teacher and coach at Ada High School before the 45th Infantry Division was called to active duty. In Korea, he served as Executive Officer of Company B, 180th Infantry Regiment.*

*(January 1952)*

*The bright red-checked shirt may have been "out of uniform" but Sergeant First Class Walter Gray of Ada, Oklahoma, often wore the shirt under his military gear to provide extra warmth. He is pictured enjoying both the sun and a hot meal in a front line position.*

*(January 1952)*
*Photo courtesy of*
*SFC Joe Hill Floyd*

*Master Sergeant Harold Gene Evans (left) of Ada, Oklahoma, was Company C's First Sergeant during the days in Japan and Korea.*

*(December 1951)*

# Chapter Four

## Fear is Powerful—

Military intelligence reports came to us daily on mimeographed printed sheets from regimental and battalion headquarters. The reports were carefully studied. Our lives could depend on that information.

The intelligence reports that were received in the days immediately following our unit's arrival at the front advised us that the main enemy body located in the hills immediately across the Yokkah-ch'on River Valley consisted of Chinese Communist Forces believed to be elements of the 39th CCF Army, the 41st CCF Army and the 47th CCF Army.

The estimated strength of those units was such that our front line companies might be outnumbered by at least a 10-to-1 ratio, perhaps even as high as a 20-to-1 ratio.

If true, and there wasn't reason to doubt the intelligence, that was scary.

In theory, an Army in the CCF was like a Corps in the American military structure, consisting of three divisions of about 10,000 men each. In reality, the actual division strength of the Chinese units was usually much smaller, later intelligence advised.

Each Chinese division, on paper, consisted of three 3000-men regiments. A normal U.S. Army division consisted of three regiments of infantry, three battalions of 105mm artillery, a battalion of 155mm artillery, an antiaircraft battalion, a tank battalion and other supporting units. Combined, the forces totaled in excess of 12,000 men.

Even if a bit under normal strength, the Chinese units that were concentrated in the area across the valley made up an impressive force. That they could fight and fight well had been established in recent months. And, our unit, even though well trained, had not been battle-tested.

In addition, personnel in our unit felt just a little bit lonely.

In December 1951, the 45th Infantry Division was scattered from the front line positions in Korea to Japan's northernmost island, Hokkaido, where the division had been stationed with a strategic defensive assignment and advanced training, and on ships in between.

Those of us in the 180th Infantry Regiment, the division's first soldiers in Korea, and its supporting units, were mixed with those from the 1st Cavalry Division as the Thunderbird division gradually replaced the 1st Cavalry Division in a "relief in place" operation that extended for almost two months.

The 180th Infantry Regiment was for the moment formed into a Regimental Combat Team, and was in the process of replacing units of the 5th Cavalry Regiment.

A time of transition can be a bit dangerous for military units.

Attached units, with good reason, sometimes felt like orphan children looking for a home.

The friendly troops that were located to the right flank of our unit was a company from the Republic of Korea (ROK) 9th Division, linking with one of Company C's rifle platoons where soldiers were scattered along the forward slopes of steep hills and in foxholes, trenches and bunkers strung out across the wide river valley.

The soldiers in Company C knew each other, had trained together in Louisiana and in Japan for many months, and had complete trust in the ability of every squad and every man, located to the right and to the left. None of us knew very much about the ROK unit located on our right flank, and, as the result did not have the same level of confidence that our flank "was covered."

There is always apprehension among soldiers in foxholes and trenches. That feeling was heightened by not knowing much about the persons, many non-English speaking, who were "covering our backside," or, in this case, "the flank."

Time would show that the apprehension was unjustified; but, during those first days on the line, our unit was extra cautious about guarding the flank—especially after hearing stories of the unique skill of the Chinese soldiers who had proven they were able to infiltrate the front lines, and to slip into foxholes, trenches and bunkers to stealthily attack soldiers who were caught off-guard.

Front line units were under orders to maintain a 50 percent alert status, especially at night. While one soldier slept, the assigned buddy looked out into the night, changing assignments, usually in two-hour shifts. When the rest time came, if a soldier considered crawling into a sleeping bag for warmth while trying to get some sleep, everyone knew not to "zip up" the sleeping bag because of the stories of infiltrators catching soldiers in sleeping bags and bayoneting the "bagged" soldier before he could defend himself.

Were we scared? You bet!

Some very wise military leader once said that anyone who claims not to be scared in combat is "both an idiot and a liar."

78

That's an accurate assessment.

There isn't anything wrong with being scared. Fear, under control, can keep a soldier alert.

During the first days in front line positions, unsure of the enemy, unsure of the friendly troops on the flank, and certainly not the battle-experienced soldiers most of us would become in the weeks ahead, everyone was nervous, and, as we soon learned, some were just a bit "trigger happy."

That nervousness became apparent one night just a few days after the unit moved into the front line positions.

In the middle of a very cold night, one rifle squad member awoke from his sleep and feeling the need to relieve himself, crawled out of his bunker, with his semi-automatic M-1 rifle in hand, and started toward an appropriate location to urinate.

In the shadows, he spotted the outline of a figure where no one was supposed to be.

"This must be an enemy soldier who had slipped by the outposts and into the unit's positions, ready to start killing, one by one, any sleeping soldiers he could find," this alert soldier reasoned.

The call for the proper password of the night failed to get a response.

He quickly flipped the safety to firing position, aimed, and cut loose with the full eight-round clip of 30-calibre ammunition. The shadowy figure absorbed the rounds and tumbled to the ground.

Certain of the deadly accuracy of his fire, he yelled, "I got him."

That seemed to be a reasonable assessment.

The firing alerted everyone in nearby foxholes, bunkers and trench locations, and all rifles were aimed into the darkness. Everyone was expecting to hear the famous "Chinese bugles," automatic weapons fire and to face a rush of enemy soldiers.

Nothing moved out front of the MLR, the main line of resistance.

All was quiet.

At the first light of dawn, the alert soldier cautiously moved toward the spot where he had noticed the figure in the night.

He found a bullet-riddled poncho that another rifleman had draped across the limbs of a scrubby bush—now in shreds on the ground.

Did the event really occur? Probably. The story was passed around among the frontline platoons, repeated many times, and most likely embellished a bit.

The name of the very eager shooter, understandably, remained anonymous.

"The fear of the Lord is the beginning of wisdom," the Psalmist once wrote.[7]

Fear of an enemy also can be the beginning of wisdom for a soldier in combat.

---

[7] Psalms, 111:10

*Climbs to the top of steep Korean hills often were measured by the number of "stops" taken to rest and catch ones breath before resuming the climb. Company C defensive positions were located on top this "six-stop" hill. Squad Leader Sergeant First Class Joe Hill Floyd (below) checks in by telephone with his platoon leader.*

*A temporary Company Command Post was among first steps taken when the unit moved into a new combat location. Using a field telephone, Master Sergeant Clarence G. Oliver, Jr., Company C's administrative officer, checks links to the company's forward platoon locations. He is seated on rolls of barbed wire that would be used to improve front line defensive positions.*

*(Spring 1952)*

# Chapter Five

## Out of the Blue—

The beautiful and sleek F-80 "Shooting Star" jet engine fighter-bombers that swooped down from the clouds to provide requested bombing runs on the Chinese positions along the hills and valleys across the front brought much-appreciated close air support to front line troops. When the pilots started the bombing and strafing runs, though, there was always a bit of uneasiness in the stomachs of those of us occupying the friendly positions.

Would the pilots spot the right hills just a few hundred yards away from very similar hills and valleys where our troops occupied a string of bunkers and trenches?

A mistake would be disastrous.

Those of us in the 180th Infantry Regiment were vaguely familiar with the "Shooting Star" jet aircraft as the result of our several months of duty and training on Japan's Hokkaido Island. After arriving in Japan as occupation troops in May 1951, the regiment established a large tent city camp outside the town of Chitose, also the location of an Air Force operational base at an airfield that during the

World War II years had been used to train Japanese Kamikaze pilots for their suicide missions.

A squadron of the Lockheed F-80 jets flew daily missions from the Chitose base as part of the strategic defense of this northernmost of the islands of Japan. Perhaps some of those jets even flew to targets in Korea. During the months of additional training in preparation for deployment to Korea, we "Thunderbirds" watched and heard the planes as they left for and returned from missions.

Now, just a few months later, our unit was benefiting from such flights, if not from airplanes flying from the Chitose air base then those from other bases in Japan and South Korea.

Infantrymen who are dug in along front line positions and in the more isolated scattered forward outposts are grateful for any additional support that may keep the enemy troops scurrying for cover. Most of that fire support was provided from some distance away—either by artillery units behind the front lines or by airplanes that drop down from the sky to provide close support to ground troops.

An infantryman on the ground can only imagine what is taking place inside the cockpit of a jet fighter-bomber that is moving at 400 to 500 miles per hour over the rugged mountainous terrain. Pilots must fly the aircraft, watch for potential enemy aircraft that might be in the area, search for a designated target area, avoid anti-aircraft fire, and then attack a specific target—with either bombs, napalm or machinegun and rocket fire.

Although the "Shooting Star" airplane was originally designed as a high-altitude interceptor, the aircraft was used extensively as a fighter-bomber in the Korean War, primarily for low-level rocket, bomb and napalm attacks against ground targets. This was the airplane that was involved in the world's first all-jet fighter air battle, when on November 8, 1950, an F-80C flown by Lieutenant Russell J. Brown, flying with the 16th Fighter-Interceptor Squadron, shot down a Russian-built MiG-15.

The airplane and the pilots were held with great respect by infantrymen.


The jet airplanes, first the F-80 "Shooting Star" that later was replaced by the faster and even more impressive North American F-86 "Sabre" jets, were the "flying machines of choice" for the Air Force. The F-80 "Shooting Star," that carried armament of six 50-calibre machine guns, eight five-inch rockets, or 2,000 pounds of bombs, could fly at a speed in excess of 500 miles per hour and could climb to an altitude of 46,000 feet. The newer "Sabre" jets could fly higher, up to 49,000 feet, and faster, up to 685 miles per hour, and carried even more rockets and bombs.

But, when it came to those screaming dives from the sky, we infantrymen along the front seemed to prefer the close air support provided by the World War II vintage Vought F-4 Corsair, a propeller driven single-seat, single-engine, carrier-based fighter-bomber used by the Navy and Marine Corps. Those Corsairs often flew at a slower speed, usually carried a heavier bomb load than the Air Force planes, and most of us on the ground felt a little more certain that the pilots could find the right ground targets a little easier.

Although the Corsairs were used extensively in Korea for ground attack and interdiction missions in support of Army troops, apparently these planes were dangerous to fly, perhaps because of the ability to fly slower and lower in support of front line ground troops. More than 320 Corsairs were lost in the Korean War due to enemy action, almost all of them to ground fire.

The jet fighters were beautiful fighting machines and impressive to watch. But, they flew fast and high. Battle lines that appear on a map do not appear as lines on the ground. A hill is a hill is a hill when viewed from a few thousand feet in the air and at 500 miles per hour. The pilots had to depend on radio instructions from someone on the ground or some other signaling device to help identify targets while at the same time attempting to spot the friendly positions on the basis of colored cloth panels that were placed on the ground in accordance with color combinations and arrangements that changed daily.

Troop identification was a critical matter. The use of bright-colored cloth panels displayed on the ground according to a "code of the day" was the established procedure for identifying the location of front line troops. Often, there was no direct communications established between the ground troops and supporting pilots. Thus, visual aids were important.

I had the responsibility each day of insuring that the platoon leaders received information about the correct "code" for displaying the colored panels to mark the friendly troop front line. One of my fears was that I would either not have the correct code or might provide erroneous code information to a platoon leader and that an incorrect display might result in an Air Force, Navy or Marine pilot dropping bombs and napalm on our positions rather than on enemy positions just a short distance away.

When the fast-moving aircraft would swoop down from the sky for close ground support, I'm sure the pilots had difficulty distinguishing one hill from another in the rugged mountain and hill country around Old Baldy, Pork Chop, T-Bone and in the Iron Triangle areas.

Years later when visiting with a veteran jet fighter pilot about the problems of such bombing runs, telling of my expressed apprehension and advising that sometimes I "held my breath" at the start of some bombing runs, I was told by the pilot that my concern was valid. Pilots did have difficulty spotting targets, and sometimes friendly troops were accidentally bombed.

Bombing runs on enemy positions consisted of the fast-moving aircraft dropping hundreds of pounds of traditional bombs and also napalm tanks. The napalm, impressive to watch from a distance of several hundred yards, blanketed an area with burning fuel that killed the enemy by the explosion, the burning, and by sucking up all the oxygen in the area.

Watching the close air support was, at times, a breathtaking experience. When napalm was used on the enemy positions, I could not avoid having strange feelings about what was going on in those enemy bunkers and trenches across the way.

Those soldiers who were suddenly engulfed with flaming napalm and whose breath was literally sucked from their lungs were "the enemy." But, they were infantrymen, just like us, serving in another Army.

Most likely, they, too, would have preferred to be home with family.

*The Lockheed F-80 Shooting Star was the United States Air Force's first operational jet fighter, making its first flight on January 8, 1944. It operated extensively in Korea in the ground attack role— primarily for low-level rocket, bomb and napalm attacks on fixed targets. Powered by a 4,600-pound static thrust Allison J33 engine, the F-80 did remarkable work at a variety of tasks in Korea.*

*Captain Garnet E. Mercer (right), commanding officer of Company C, 180ᵗʰ Infantry Regiment, with Master Sergeant Clarence G. Oliver, Jr.*

*(February 1952.)*

# Chapter Six

## Hot Shower and More—

Nothing can make a person appreciate a hot shower more than not bathing for more than a month.

Going without a shower or bath, other than a hurried splash bath using an inverted steel helmet, gives a person a greater appreciation for the opportunity to stand under a stream of warm water.

A soldier can get a bit grungy—even if that time is during a season of sub-freezing weather.

After a month-long front line assignment that included trudging the hills and valleys along the MLR west of Ch'orwan, and sleeping in dank trenches and bunkers, small numbers of soldiers were pulled out of place for a few hours and transported to a rear area location along the banks of a small mountain stream where a Quartermaster unit had established a field shower facility by converting squad tents into temporary shower rooms.

The arrangements were very ingenious, even if a bit unrefined in design.

The shower facility consisted of a double row pipe system with clusters of showerheads suspended inside the tent and connected by hoses to a nearby water trailers, holding tanks, heating units and pumps that pulled water from the nearby stream, heated the water and then pumped the hot water into the tent.

I don't know who engineered the design, but it was effective and greatly appreciated.

The units responsible for the showers had their own problems to face. One major operational problem—muddy water—sometimes forced the bath units to shut down at times in order to prolong the life of the equipment.

Sedimentation, filtration and sterilization equipment often was available to clean up the muddy water problem—but, not always. Just how to deal with the problem was described in a memo passed along from some higher command headquarters staff. The solution offered was for the teams operating the bath units to dig holes on nearby higher ground to a depth below the stream level, with the idea that holes are near enough to the source of water so that by a process of filtration muddy water seeping through the sand and rocks would provide clean water for baths.

That seemed easy enough, except for the soldiers who had to dig the holes.

The often sandy Korean soil had a tendency to "cave in." Some bath unit teams reinforced the holes with rock, or sheets of tin, but sand caved in behind and got in underneath, and the water in the holes was as muddy as the water in the stream.

For a guy who hasn't had a shower for several weeks, a little murky water didn't seem to be that much of an issue. Even with slightly muddy water a possibility, a hot shower was a nice treat.

After a short truck ride in open trucks, the "unclean" jumped stiffly out of the "six-bys," the two and one-half-ton all purpose trucks with six-wheel drive systems that proved to be the standby transportation for infantry troops, and then headed toward a large tent. The instructions were to "strip down"—all the way—disposing of the rank clothes with the promise that clean clothes would be provided after the shower.

That promise was kept.

After enjoying the first real bath in over a month, the squeaky clean troopers exited the shower tent into an adjacent tent where clean underwear and uniforms were provided.

The feel of a clean body and clean clothes brought a vast improvement in morale of individuals.

Then, it was back to the trucks and back to the front.

Nothing like a hot shower in the morning before going off to work!

### *Mickey Mouse Boots, Etcetera—*

Combat clothing was issued to each of us in the days prior to leaving Japan for Korea. Included in our supply of winter gear were such things as wool underwear, leather gloves with wool glove inserts, thick wool socks, field pants to wear over wool pants, pile jackets, pile caps, parkas and shoepacs—a holdover cold weather footgear developed and used in the later days of World War II winter fighting in Europe.

Soldiers thrust into the battles in Korea during the early stages of the war for the most part were equipped much the same as were soldiers toward the end of World War II that had ended just five years earlier.

Even by the start of the second Korean winter when Company C joined in the battle, some clothing and equipment deficiencies continued. Clothing, equipment and supplies left over from the last days of World War II were issued to the Korea-bound troops.

During the late 1940s, after experiencing the difficulties of fighting a war under challenging winter weather conditions in Europe, the United States Army had started developing new equipment for cold weather combat conditions. In time, some of the experimental clothing and equipment items were tried out by troops fighting in Korea.

For the most part, though, during the start of the second year of the Korean War, the World War II leftover equipment was in the Army's warehouses and used in Korea. That situation was rather evident by looking at the packaging dates on ammunition and food, most of which clearly indicated that many items were packaged during the closing years of the previous war. The cans of beans, hash, corned beef, crackers and other items issued as the well-known C-rations (Combat rations) usually were marked with 1944 packaging dates. The same was true of ammunition supplies.

Despite that fact that the items were "canned" a few years earlier, the food was acceptable, and at times, even rather good. That quality evaluation, though, may have been influenced by just how hungry one might have been.

A shortage of supplies was common and obtaining some replacement winter gear at times was difficult. New winter clothing and equipment was developed by the Army and began to arrive in the supply chain—usually in small quantities, and rarely enough to meet the needs. Front line troops—Infantry rifle companies—were at the end of a long supply chain and often were the last to get the newest issue.

One example of shortage was that Company C was issued only enough white camouflage suits to equip one rifle platoon when a combat patrol or attack mission was conducted over snow-covered terrain. When a platoon returned from a mission, the camouflage suits were collected and issued to another platoon for the next mission.

Most units were equipped with a mixture of cold weather uniform items. Supply sergeants were eager to locate and obtain new uniforms and equipment to replace items that became damaged or lost.

This new war provided the Army with the conditions to test new equipment and uniform items in real combat conditions. One of the experimental items was the new winter footgear—something eagerly anticipated by Infantrymen.

The old World War II wet-cold M-1944 shoepac, with rubber foot and leather upper, proved to be inadequate in Korea. It was very poorly designed for cold weather operations. But, for the present, that was the best that the Army could provide.

Two pairs of one-half inch thick flat felt inserts, or soles, were issued with each pair of shoepacs. During the weeks of coldest weather, most of us wore two pairs of wool socks, with one pair of the inserts placed on the bottoms inside each boot. The other pair of inserts was to be placed next to the skin, generally one under each armpit or near the stomach, along with a pair of wool socks, to keep them dry.

The felt inserts in the boot were supposed to capture the moisture from foot perspiration. The felt inserts, usually frozen stiff after a few hours from absorbed moisture, had to be changed regularly—at least daily. The same was true for the wool socks.

Keeping one pair of felt inserts "thawed" for replacement use was an absolute necessity to avoid frostbitten feet. When felt inserts were changed, the moisture-soaked, frozen inserts were placed inside our clothing, against our skin, to be "thawed" by body heat and made ready for the next replacement.

The process was crude, but effective.

Although the shoepacs proved to be better winter footwear than just plain leather combat boots, most of us eagerly-awaited the arrival of a new boot that was reported to be "on the way" to troops in Korea.

As was true for much of the new equipment, though, the second Korean winter was almost over before the first shipment of the new boots arrived and some of Company C's soldiers got to "try out" the new winter footgear.

Infantrymen who are serving in front line positions are good critics.

During February 1952, Company C received a small supply of the "Mickey Mouse" boots, enough to equip soldiers in one rifle platoon. Just as was the case with the white camouflage suits, the new insulated combat boots were traded around among the platoons when a platoon was given a combat patrol or attack mission. Upon return, the new boots were issued to the soldiers in the next platoon. Spring arrived before enough "Mickey Mouse" boots were available to equipment the entire company.

The new footwear was a rubber-insulated combat boot that was large and thick, designed with rubber inner and outer surface, with insulating material between the layers.

Soldiers quickly gave the new boots names such as "Mickey Mouse," "Korean boot" and "K-boots." Some soldiers who had the mistaken notion that rabbit fur was the insulation also called those boots "Bunny Boots."

Not true.

The interior was wool-lined, with several layers of rubber to serve as insulation. Some of these boots were tinted white to camouflage with snow, but most were standard black issue.

These boots did keep a soldier's feet warm, however they also kept feet wet, a condition that required soldiers to dry their feet every night, to put on dry socks and use foot powder in order to control fungus growth and infections.

There are times and conditions when an Infantry soldier may find it a little difficult to pull off his boots, dry his feet, use foot powder, put on clean dry socks, and slip back in to the bulbous insulated boots.

Since the rubber boot, which reached halfway up the calf, wasn't ventilated in any way, the wearer's sweat collected quickly. Men were constantly changing their socks, and drying wet socks between layers of their clothing.

The boots prevented frostbite, though, even when the temperature dropped to the 20 degrees below zero level that occurred in Korea. A thin layer of air trapped between two layers of rubber acts as a powerful insulator. A greater problem was that the weight and bulk of "Mickey Mouse" boots adversely affected a person's mobility, and weren't comfortable for long treks.

Some liked the new "Mickey Mouse" boots. Some did not hold them in high regard.

Regardless of opinion, though, by Spring 1952, that was the new combat footgear for the soldier in Korea.


News that the Army had developed a new cold weather tent—a winter cousin of the famous "pup tent"—was of great interest to those of us in Infantry units. One of the tents was reported to have been on display at the division headquarters before our unit departed Japan for Korea, but none of us saw the tent.

Rumors persisted that the tents would be delivered to units in Korea. As was true with the "Mickey Mouse" boots, front line units seemed to be at the end of the supply chain. Company C did receive two or three of the Hexagon tents in late February 1952 and Master Sergeant George McCorkle and I were privileged to share one of the new tents.

A great deal of thought went into the design of the Hexagon tent. The tent had an inner, white lining that reflected light better than the usual olive drab color. Aluminum tent pegs and a center pole were lightweight for easier carrying. And, miracle of all miracles, each tent kit included a small, gasoline Yukon stove. That was great if one could scrounge around and get some gasoline.

The tent's hexagonal (six-sided) teepee shape could withstand strong winds, and snow was easily shed from the top. A ground cloth around the bottom kept out the cold wind and kept the warm air inside.

The tent did not have a floor, but unlike the two-part "pup tent" that had been the Infantryman's shelter for several years, the Hexagon tent was high enough to permit a person to stand in the center.

Although one soldier's evaluation wasn't stated in the best English grammar, his comment, "the Army done good," was an accurate assessment of the opinion most of us had about the new tent.

The tent wasn't practical for use in areas where soldiers were in direct combat with the enemy, but for time spent in reserve locations or in other safer areas, the Hexagon tent was great.

Unlike the two-part "pup tent," carrying the Hexagon tent was a bit more difficult for a foot march.


Infantrymen are known for being able to "adapt" to whatever conditions they must endure.

Life goes on.

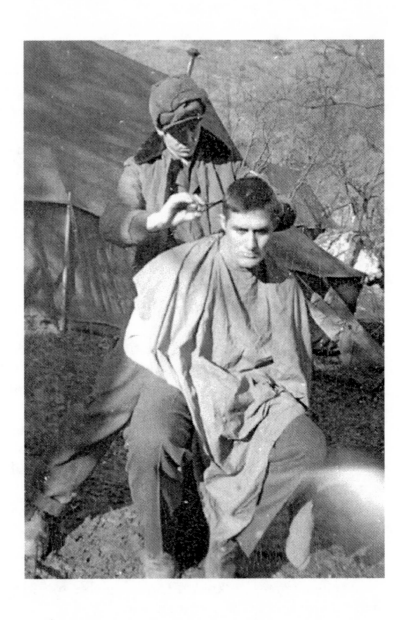

*Korea Barber Shop: Sergeant James A. Kimrey of Ada, Oklahoma, gives his friend Sergeant First Class James A. West, also of Ada, a proper trim during time in reserve location.*
*(March 1952)*

*The Army developed new cold weather equipment in the years after World War II, but some of the promised new innovative items, such as the Hexagon tent, the winter tent to replace "pup tents," didn't reach soldiers in Korea until Spring 1952. Master Sergeant George McCorkle (right) and Master Sergeant Clarence G. Oliver, Jr., shared a new Hexagon tent in a reserve location.*

*(March 1952)*

# Chapter Seven

## By Candlelight—

Being many miles from any source of artificial light when nighttime comes makes one realize what "dark" means, especially when any natural light from the stars and moon is obscured by heavy clouds.

On clear nights, the celestial bodies provide a surprising amount of natural light that permits careful movement and observation for soldiers occupying foxholes, trenches and bunkers in a combat zone. There were times, though, when some source of light was needed inside concealed combat zone bunkers for reading and preparation of reports—but not always for such official work. After all, if time and conditions permitted, three or four friends might gather in a protected bunker area simply to talk or work in a card game to pass the hours when "all is quiet" along the front.

Finding some source of "light" to use inside concealed bunkers was important. Infantry soldiers are accustomed to "making do" with whatever is available in the performance of duty. That proved true in the search for any source of artificial light. One innovative radio operator determined that the batteries used to power the SCR-300 radios, a hefty 50-pound backpack radio that was used as a communication link with outposts and for patrol operations, could be wired to an electric light socket and bulb, and provide excellent lighting—for a while.

Those primary radio batteries were the "use it once and throw it away" variety. Battery life was drained quickly when used to power light bulbs. After a few supply orders for new radio batteries raised the question from battalion and regimental supply officers about why our unit was using up so many batteries, that source of lighting was ended.

It was a great idea, but the batteries were needed for the intended purpose of the critical radio communications with outposts, patrols and combat missions. So, the brief period of a having an "electric" light in a bunker came to an abrupt end.

The most logical light source was the use of candles—any size, shape or form would do. Candles became a precious commodity, carefully rationed and used sparingly.

My wonderful wife, Vinita, tried to provide a steady supply of candles in "care packages" that she frequently mailed to us. Candles of various sizes and shapes were received. The favorite size was about one-inch in diameter, three or four inches in height.

Administrative tasks required my performing some daily paperwork, morning reports, the commanding officer's correspondence and typed operational orders. Most of that work was done within the confines of a bunker, working at a portable field desk and using a portable Remington typewriter.

Thus, I used up my supply of candles quickly.

Corporal Don Peterson, a teacher from South Dakota before he received his "Greetings" from President Truman inviting him to join us in military service, was my very able assistant as company clerk. He and I decided that some "homemade" candles might do the trick, and began thinking about how candles could be created.

What could we use for wicks and a soft material that would slowly melt with the heat from a burning wick?

Ah ha! The Army supplied butter in one-gallon cans. What about using butter?

That seemed reasonable to us. We "requisitioned" a can of butter from the cooks.

Our theory was that a gallon can of butter could be converted into a big candle that would burn for days, and surely would supply our Company Command Post bunker with good candlelight.

A wick of appropriate dimension to match the six-inch diameter "butter candle" seemed in order. The only likely item we could find was some 1/4-inch cotton tent rope. Thus, we two candlemakers carefully inserted an eight-inch piece of rope into the one-gallon can of butter, rubbed some butter on the exposed tip of the rope-wick, and prepared to enjoy the light of this massive candle.

With great fanfare, a match was struck and the flame was carefully placed to the wick.

The flame flickered. Smoke came forth.


There is more to "making a candle" than sticking a wick of appropriate diameter in the center of something that will melt.

Butter melts, but it smokes and stinks.

What a mess!

Later, we would-be candlemakers learned about such fine candle making skills as melt points, choosing the "best" candle wick, essentially a balancing act between the type and size of the candle and the formula used.

Too late, I learned that everything from the diameter of the candle to the type of material used could affect the type of wick needed for a clean-burning candle; and that candles normally are made using paraffin waxes, beeswax, or some soy-blend waxes.

Butter didn't have the needed characteristics. That fact was learned through our smoky trial and error experiment.

Two reasonably intelligent and college-educated guys should have known better.

It seemed like a good idea. Big mistake.

So much for being innovative candlemakers!

*Corporal Donald Peterson of Sioux Falls, South Dakota, Company Clerk, at work in Company C's command post.*

*He was one of the "infamous" candle-makers.*

*(February 1952)*

*Ice and snow blanketed the area during much of January and February 1952. Below, Sergeant First Class Paul N. Scott of Ada, Oklahoma, uses a pickaxe in an effort to clear the entrance to the unit's supply tent.*

*Company C's snow-covered Command Post area, west of Ch'orwan, North Korea. Master Sergeant Clarence G. Oliver, Jr., at field desk handling administrative tasks by candlelight.*
*(December 1951)*

# Chapter Eight

## Restful Night in Yongdungp'o—

During the early months of the war, the battles were fought on almost every part of the Korean peninsula. By the start of what became the battle period known as the "Second Korean Winter," the war was limited mostly along a line across the middle of the land, somewhat north of the 38th parallel as an effort was made to move toward some form of negotiated settlement.

In the meantime, the fighting continued.

The business of war—the skirmishes, probes, attacks to take some perceived critical hill or to defend some valued terrain, the artillery and aerial bombardments, the propaganda efforts of both armies, the deaths of friends and wounding of others—consumed our lives, day and night.

As the person charged with administrative responsibilities for the unit, I found it necessary to visit the regimental personnel section to resolve some questions related to unit records, and discussed with Captain Mercer the plan to drive to the division rear headquarters area to complete the needed work.

The personnel section was located in the city of Yongdungp'o, near Seoul, the capital of South Korea, about 90 miles from our front line positions. The trip and the business at hand would require a full day, if all went according to plan.

Captain Mercer decided to use the trip to take care of another matter that had come to his attention—a "paperwork problem" related to one of the Korean Service Corps (KSC) members from the unit attached to support Company C.

One of the older men in the Korean Service Corps unit was a refugee from North Korea who had escaped with his family to South Korea before the war erupted in June 1950. His name was Kim—a very common Korean family name that might be considered similar to "Smith" or "Jones" in America. At times it seemed that half the Korean population was named "Kim."

The Koreans in the KSC provided valuable manpower support for the American forces, freeing more men for true combat roles. In addition to providing daily supply support, KSC members frequently accompanied units on combat patrols, serving as litter bearers to carry wounded soldiers back to the friendly positions to receive medical aid.

Through the KSC communications channels, Kim was advised of the need to report to a South Korean political office in Seoul to clarify papers related to his presence in South Korea and the KSC service with the 45th Infantry Division.

Captain Mercer decided to send Kim along with us on the trip to the Seoul area, and instructed us to assist him, if necessary, in resolving any issues related to his assignment in support of Company C.

Sergeant First Class Paul Scott, the unit's supply sergeant and a close personal friend, was asked to accompany us on the trip and to assist with driving.

The three of us left in an open Jeep in weather that was reported to be several degrees below zero. The trip to Seoul, over very difficult terrain, required six or seven hours—longer than anticipated.


Soldiers can be ingenious in dealing with day-by-day life in a combat zone. Little things can make a difference.

Finding a way to thaw and then warm up frozen cans of C-rations that we carried for our lunch and dinner for the day on the road was a concern. Recalling advice from one of the unit's drivers, Sergeant Scott used some strands of wire to tie C-ration cans to the Jeep engine's manifold so the cans of pork and beans and hash would be warm to eat.

Surprisingly, it worked. The cans did not overheat. Otherwise, an explosion would have splattered our lunch and dinner over the entire engine compartment—and left us hungry.


The trip to Seoul, Yongdungp'o and return would take us across the 38th parallel—going and returning.

The 38th parallel doesn't appear as a line on the ground.

Officially, the parallel is an imaginary circle of latitude that is 38 degrees north of the Earth's equatorial plane, and the parallel passes across oceans and seas and through countries all around the world.

In the United States, the parallel extends from the Pacific Ocean across California, Nevada, Utah, Colorado, Kansas, Missouri, Illinois, Indiana, Kentucky, West Virginia and Maryland and then into the Atlantic Ocean.

But, the 38th parallel north was especially important in the history of Korea after the end of World War II. Those of us who fought in the Korean War truly learned the importance of that "line."

At the end of World War II, with the surrender of Japan, the $38^{th}$ parallel was a convenient dividing boundary across the Korean peninsula to divide the Soviet occupied area and interests in the north and the United States occupied area and interests in the south. The parallel ran approximately through the middle of the Korean peninsula.

When the Korean War ended in 1953 after extensive negotiations, the Demilitarized Zone (DMZ) was established to divide North and South Korea. The DMZ cuts across the $38^{th}$ parallel at an angle, from southwest to northeast—sometimes below and sometimes above the $38^{th}$ parallel.

But on the cold winter day of the trip to Yongdungp'o, the $38^{th}$ parallel was an important line on the map.


The South Korean capitol building was a gutted shell of a building. That building and much of the city were left in ruins by the see-saw battles over the City of Seoul as first the North Korean Army attacked and occupied the city in June 1950, then the U. S. Army recaptured the city in October 1950, lost again to the Chinese and North Koreans in January 1951, and finally recaptured and held by the U. S. Army in March 1951.

Occupation of Seoul had changed hands four times within a year, and the city was in ruins. Once a city of 1.5 million people, the population had been reduced to approximately 200,000. In the months that followed, people began to return to the city and to re-establish what was once a great city.

Because of the devastation of the Capitol and many other government buildings, most South Korean government offices were scattered throughout the area.

Kim had been given a street address, but finding an address in a war-damaged city of nearly a half-million or more people was a real challenge for two American soldiers whose knowledge of the Korean language was extremely limited.

After some difficulty, and depending almost entirely on the efforts of Kim, the remote office was finally located in an area of Seoul that had not been totally destroyed by the fighting during the previous year.

The office was found in a ramshackle one-story building with mud-covered brick walls, boarded windows and a wooden door that swung open directly into the small office area. Kim and I entered the room and were met by three Korean men that I assumed to be the political officials who could deal with the questions and paperwork that Kim needed to complete.

None of the men spoke English, or none would acknowledge an understanding of the language. Kim entered into lengthy discussion with the three men, who continued to shuffle several documents that seemed to relate to the situation.

Eventually, Kim handed me two or three pages of documents that he said related to confirmation that he was in fact serving with the KSC unit that was attached to our front line unit, and said that the papers needed the signature of the commanding officer.

What to do?

Captain Garnet E. Mercer, commanding officer of Company C, was 90 miles or so away, and obviously not available to sign these papers.

As the unit's administrative officer, I had on occasion been authorized by Captain Mercer to sign his name to routine papers, reports and correspondence that I had prepared for him when circumstances made it difficult for him to return promptly to the company command post bunker simply for a signature.

To a casual observer, my version of the commanding officer's signature could easily pass for the genuine article. The Korean officials did not know my identity and assumed that this tall man in an American Army uniform and armed with a 45-caliber pistol displayed in a shoulder holster must be the commander. Kim handed me the papers. I reached inside my parka and pulled forth a Parker 51 fountain pen that I used for signatures and, with a flourish, signed on each document, "Garnet E. Mercer, Captain, Infantry, U. S. Army."

The Korean men nodded, smiled, politely bowed and then shook hands with us. Kim was advised that he could leave.

Signing papers that were written in a foreign language that I did not understand may not have been the smartest thing to do. The emergency nature of the situation seemed to require such action, though, in order to get permission for Kim to remain in his assignment with the KSC, a role that provided regular income for him and his small refuge family living in Seoul.

Apparently the signature and papers were found to be acceptable, and no one ever questioned the act.

Kim indicated he planned to remain in Seoul for a visit with his family and that he would find transportation back to the unit in a day or two through his KSC contacts.

He walked off down a narrow street.


The shadows of a Korean winter evening were beginning as Sergeant Scott and I—unexpectedly delayed a few hours—climbed back into the Jeep to continue our drive to Yongdungp'o to find the location of the 45th Division's rear headquarters, and to complete some official business in a language I could understand.

Our specific search was to find the regimental personnel section, a part of the 180th Infantry Regiment's Service Company. Sergeant Scott and I returned to the Jeep and headed toward the nearby city of Yongdungp'o.

The various administrative offices, supply facilities, and mixture of other service organizations were housed mostly in a collection of old warehouse and industrial buildings that had survived earlier battles back and forth through the Seoul area, or had been repaired sufficiently to be used.

The city of Yongdungp'o might be described as an industrial suburb of Seoul, and is located just across the Han River, west and southwest of South Korea's capital city. During the initial weeks of the war, Yongdungp'o was one of the major objectives of the North Korean army since the city was considered to be key to the road and rail network leading south.

The city's infrastructure was heavily damaged.


There is a side of war and of soldiers that is vastly different from the battle stories told in so many Hollywood-style productions. Special relationships develop among people who are thrust together in unusual situations.

People who serve together in a military unit during wartime often bond together with a unique friendship that is difficult to describe and that can endure for a lifetime.

The trip to Yongdungp'o would contribute to one such friendship.

The personnel section sergeant who welcomed us into his warehouse office was Sergeant First Class Kinney E. Coleman whose hometown was Okemah, Oklahoma. The two of us had become acquainted during the days of working together on personnel matters while stationed in

Louisiana and Japan, prior to the deployment to Korea. A friendship was building.

Sergeant Coleman had enlisted in Service Company, 180th Infantry Regiment, after graduating from high school, signing up to serve under the command of one of the community's leading citizens.

Colonel James O. Smith, commander of the 180th Infantry Regiment, was a prominent businessman and community leader in Okemah. He was the owner of a large hardware store. Colonel Smith had a long history with this unit he now commanded. He had enlisted in Company D, 180th Infantry Regiment, as a youth in 1920 and rose through the ranks to become first sergeant and then was appointed a second lieutenant in 1940 not long before the 45th Infantry Division was called to active duty for World War II.

When the "Thunderbirds" shipped out for overseas service in the early days of World War II, the young soldier was company commander. He served with distinction with the regiment and was one of the most respected infantry officers in the division. By the end of the war he was a battalion commander.

In 1946, when the 45th Infantry Division was being reorganized, Colonel Smith was named commander of the historic regiment in which he had enlisted as a young private so many years earlier. He was proud of the 180th Infantry Regiment, and that feeling was instilled into all of us who served in that unit with him and under his command.

Colonel Smith was a leader who loved to create mottos and slogans for the men he led. When the 45th Division was called to active duty in 1950, Colonel Smith announced that the unit's current slogan was "Let's Get With It!"

And, all of us did just that.

When the 180th Regimental Combat Team was formed and deployed to Korea, Colonel Smith said the new slogan was to be, the 180th is "The Cleanest and Meanest."

The "Warrior" Regiment embraced that motto, already believing that "we were the meanest" Infantry unit in Korea, and now with a new sense of pride in cleanliness, even in challenging combat assignments.

Colonel Smith had been "in the thick of battle" as an Infantryman in a rifle company and as an Infantry officer, and he was close to the men he led.

As can occur in small towns, the Sergeant and the Colonel were close friends.


Sergeant Coleman assisted us in completing the updating of records and other administrative tasks that first prompted the trip, and then suggested that we take some time to look around the area.

Nighttime was upon us.


## Meeting "the Brits"

Our unofficial host for the evening, Sergeant Coleman, advised us that some British soldiers were stationed in a nearby area. He had become friends with the British soldiers and wanted us to meet those new friends from England.

The invitation was quickly accepted.

The British soldiers were "tankers," proud members of a tank squadron from the British Commonwealth forces. The British have a long history of success in tank warfare, including many battles in North Africa and Europe during World War II. The new acquaintances were eager to talk about that history—and their unit.

The British tankers were spirited soldiers. They, also, were from a great unit in an Army from another country.

Their squadron was equipped with the famous British Centurion tank that had been developed in 1944 during the closing year of World War II. The Centurion—a 57-ton monster more than 25-feet long, almost 12-feet wide, and armed with a 105-mm main gun and three machine guns— was now the United Kingdom's main battle tank,

They were prepared to enter into tank battles, either in an attack or in other front line battle opportunities. Neither was to happen for them during this time of the war in Korea. They were given a defense and reserve mission, with positions far behind the front lines, but ready for instant deployment.

Few open tank battles ever occurred, though, during the Korean War. Unlike the desert areas of North Africa or some of the open, flat lands in Europe, tanks were unable to efficiently move around in the mountainous regions of Korea.

The tanks could be set up in reserve positions to be called into action if needed, or placed on hills or cliffs and used to provide direct fire support for front line troops.

The Centurion Tank Squadron was deployed in a reserve position near the South Korean capital, available for quick deployment in support of the defense of any of the major Army units currently holding the shifting front line positions.

Each Centurion tank carried a crew of five men— and we had just become acquainted with one such crew of very interesting young men from England. They were eager to talk about England, themselves and their families. To say that they were "proud" of their country, their unit and their tanks would be an understatement.

Theirs was a great unit, and they knew it.

Spending a few hours listening to and talking with the British soldiers was a most enjoyable time.

It is true—they do enjoy a cup of tea, among other drinks.

*The sign says it all. Sergeant First Class Paul N. Scott (right) and Master Sergeant Clarence G. Oliver, Jr., stop at the 38th Parallel on a return to front line positions after a trip to Seoul and Yongdungp'o. Below, the two are pictured near the war-gutted South Korean Capitol building in Seoul. (January 1952)*

The British tank squadron was just one of the many units from other countries that gathered in support of South Korea in this battle to save this young nation.

Most of the military forces in Korea were from the United States. But, the "Brits" we had become acquainted with were part of the forces that made up the largest non-U.S. contribution to the war effort—the British First Commonwealth Division. That division was organized in 1951 from British army battalions and similar units from Canada, Australia and New Zealand and dispatched to Korea.

An impressive coalition of United Nations forces came to the aid of South Korea in response to the invasion by North Korea in June 1950. In addition to the United States and South Korea, 14 other nations placed some military forces under the United Nations command.

The ground forces included a Canadian brigade, Turkish brigade, New Zealand field artillery regiment, and battalions from France, Thailand, Ethiopia, Greece, the Philippines, Belgium, Australia, Colombia and the Netherlands.

An unlikely participant was the mid-East country of Turkey that committed more than 5,000 troops with the Turkish Brigade. The unit operated under the U.S. 25th Infantry Division and earned a reputation and a great deal of praise for the heroic fighting in the battles of Kunu-ri and Kumyanjangni.

The country that sent the smallest unit to the war effort was Luxembourg, with one platoon committed to the battle.

Five nations—Denmark, India, Italy, Norway and Sweden—sent only medical units.

North Korea was aided by the Soviet Union (USSR) and allied with Communist China.

With a few exceptions—most notably the heroic action of the British Commonwealth units and the Turkish brigade—most of the non-U.S. and Republic of Korea forces did not have significant impact on the operational courses of the war.

Although all of us knew there were military units from several nations joined in the war effort under the United Nations command, our contact with them was almost non-existent. The 9$^{th}$ ROK (Republic of South Korea) Division was linked to our company on the right flank during December 1951. No other non-U.S. unit was around us.

The enjoyable visit with the "Brits" ended late that Korean winter night. Saying "Goodbye" to these new friends was awkward since all of us knew that most likely none of us would ever meet again—at least in this lifetime.

As Sergeants Coleman, Scott and I slowly walked back toward his office area, our discussion shifted from the visit with the British soldiers to my inquiry about where we "might sleep" that night. Sergeant Coleman suggested that his office area might be a good spot. He offered the office floor.

Amenities such as cots and sleeping bags simply were not available. Sergeant Scott and I had not brought sleeping bags with us since in our original planning; this was to have been a one-day trip. The delays of the day had not been anticipated.

The office floor in the personnel section was to be our bed for the night.

The personnel section was located in an old warehouse building, one with ancient wood floors, no insulation, windows that rattled as the winter wind blew, and was warmed by a pot-bellied oil heater located in the center of the room.

Nothing fancy. But, it was late at night.

I plopped down on the wood floor, stretched out next to the oil burner stove with only my parka for a bed and cover, and had the most comfortable, restful, peaceful night's sleep of all the nights in Korea.

I was warm, well fed and safe. No mortar rounds were exploding. There was no threat of enemy attack.

For the moment, I had few worries.


Sergeant First Class Coleman was a man I didn't see again for 14 years.

He appeared one night at a board of education meeting in Broken Arrow, Oklahoma, where I was serving as assistant superintendent of schools. He was an applicant to serve as an architect for Broken Arrow Public Schools to design a proposed new school—one that is now Sequoyah Middle School.

When he walked into the meeting room that night, my mind jumped back a few years. That was the same man I had known in Army days in the United States, Japan and Korea.

Hundreds of images flashed through my mind and memories of that wartime friendship were recalled at the time of this somewhat emotional reunion. The friendship of long ago was renewed.

Kinney Coleman and his associate, Bill Schneider, that night were contracted to design and coordinate the construction of a planned new Sequoyah Middle School in Broken Arrow. During the years that followed, that architectural team designed and coordinated the construction of most of the new school buildings, major additions to others, and the development of more than 20 new school campuses in Broken Arrow from 1965 until Coleman's death in 2000.


This friendship formed in wartime lasted a lifetime.

Kinney Coleman wrote about that friendship more than a half-century later in a letter delivered to me after his death on December 30, 2000. The letter was hand-written on a yellow legal tablet and dated "Veterans Day, November 1, 1997."

My friend had written the letter more than three years before its delivery to me, apparently not long after he learned that the treatment for prostate cancer that had been diagnosed earlier was not progressing as expected, and that the disease most likely would cause an early death.

He began with these words: "It is appropriate to write this letter on Veterans Day since it was through the military that we met."

He told of the friendship that began in our days together in military service in the 45th Infantry Division and the very special friendship, the trust, the mutual respect that was felt during the 30 years of working together—he as the architect and I, as the school administrator—building schools in Broken Arrow, Oklahoma.

Kinney Coleman ended the letter with these words, "Thank you for being my friend."

The mutual feelings of absolute trust, genuine affection and unconditional support between friends are difficult to describe.

Such a friendship is rare.

Kinney Coleman and I enjoyed that kind of a relationship.

I was blessed.

*Sergeant First Class Paul N. Scott (right) and Master Sergeant Clarence G. Oliver, Jr., are pictured outside the warehouse buildings in Yongdungp'o, near Seoul, where the 180th Infantry Regiment's Personnel Section and other "rear headquarters" offices were located. Oliver is sporting a 45-calibre pistol in a shoulder holster.*

*(January 1952)*

*Fifty years after the "Restful Night in Yongdungp'o" and their war-time service in Korea, Kinney E. Coleman (center), his wife, Nina, and Clarence G. Oliver, Jr., share memories during a 1992 community-wide reception held to recognize Oliver upon his retirement as Superintendent of Broken Arrow (Oklahoma) Public Schools. During Oliver's 30 years as a Broken Arrow administrator, Coleman and his architect partner, Bill Schneider, designed and supervised construction of three dozen buildings on more than 20 new school campuses in Broken Arrow—including the multi-million dollar Oliver Middle School that was built after Oliver's retirement.*

# Chapter Nine

## The Combat Infantryman—

There is something very special about an Infantry soldier. Historic Fort Benning, Georgia, considered as the "Home of the Infantry," is the site of the United States Army's Infantry School. A tour of duty—or even a visit—to that post gives a person a greater understanding of the history of the Infantry branch of service and the traditions that Infantry soldiers hold dear.

The Infantry is described at that school and elsewhere as "The Queen of Battle," a reflection of the most valued and most powerful of chess pieces, the very versatile Queen, the only chess piece that can move and attack in any direction.

With few exceptions, most armies in history have been built around a core of Infantry. Weapons may have varied, but the common factor is that these soldiers have fought "on the ground," often relying on their own two feet for operational movement in close combat.

Here is how the Infantry is revered by those who wear and have worn the "Crossed Rifles" of Infantry:

## The Queen of Battle

*We are members of one of the oldest professions in the history of the world. However, from time immemorial critics, historians and conquerors have looked askance at the lowly foot soldier. Ingenious minds have long endeavored to conceive something to replace us. From the forgotten soul who invented the chariot, to the development of the modern panzer division of tanks, one idea has ruled the trend of war— crush the Infantry. But we have replied — Abela, Crecy, Guadalajara and Stalingrad are ours. We have a heritage that is equaled by none. We do not have the glamour that the public has spread over the Air Corps or the Navy; nor are we a specialized task force as are the Marines. We are—the Doughboy, the Dogface, the Poilu and the Tommy; the men who dig, fight and die; the jack-of-all-trades; the men who must and will win all conflicts. We are the riflemen who proudly wear the crossed rifles, we will surmount all obstacles and all barriers, alone and unaided if need be. For we are — THE INFANTRY.*[8]

An Infantry rifle company is the true essence of "The Infantry." Although the mission of an Infantry division, regiment, battalion or a company is the same, the rifle company is the unit that most often is called on to execute that mission of "closing with the enemy by means of fire and maneuver in order to destroy, capture, or repel their assault by fire, close combat, and counterattack."

The distinguished historian Stephen E. Ambrose wrote extensively about Infantry soldiers and rifle compa-

---

[8] The United States Army Infantry School, Fort Benning, Georgia (1943)
<https://www.benning.army.mil/infantry/>

nies in his books, *Band of Brothers* and *D-Day June 6, 1941: The Climactic Battle of World War II*. He had these special words to say about an Infantry rifle company:

> *"Within the ranks of the military, a rifle company is unique. Its prolonged exposure to the horrors of face-to-face combat forges bonds that are virtually unbreakable. With closeness unknown to all outsiders, comrades are closer than friends, closer than brothers. Their relationship is different from that of lovers. Their trust in, and knowledge of, each other is total."*[9]

In recognition of the unique role that the front-line soldier plays in carrying out combat missions, the then War Department during World War II created a special award for the infantrymen who were acknowledged to have continuously operated under the worst conditions and performed a mission that was not assigned to any other soldier or unit.

Thus was created the Combat Infantryman Badge—the CIB—that was originally proposed to be called the "Fighter Badge" when first recommended by Lieutenant General Lesley J. McNair, then the Army Ground Forces commanding general, who was instrumental in its creation.

Although formally established in early 1943, authorization for the award of the CIB was backdated to December 6, 1941, to be earned for action under hostel fire while engaged with an enemy of the United States of America, when the United States is not the belligerent party.

The Combat Infantryman Badge was designed to enhance morale and the prestige of the "Queen of Battle."

That goal was achieved.

---

[9] Ambrose (1992)
<http://www.104infdiv.org/tribute.htm>

Those who have earned the right to wear the CIB—a silver and enamel badge, one inch in height and three inches in width, consisting of an infantry musket on a light blue bar with a silver border and on an elliptical oak wreath—do so with honor and pride.

Few awards hold greater respect among those who serve or have served in the military.

I once overheard Lieutenant Colonel Ernest Childers tell a group of middle school students at Ernest Childers Middle School in Broken Arrow, Oklahoma, how much he revered the CIB that he was awarded in World War II. A recipient of the Medal of Honor, the nation's highest award for valor, Colonel Childers told the students that he prized the CIB "almost as much" as the Medal of Honor.

That comment may have been a bit of an exaggeration on the part of this great hero, but he obviously was extremely proud that he had been awarded the unique badge of a Combat Infantryman.

The symbolism of the badge is unique. The bar is blue, the color associated with the Infantry branch of service. The musket is adapted from the Infantry insignia of branch and represents the first official shoulder arm of the United States—the 1795 model Springfield Arsenal musket that was adopted as the official Infantry branch insignia in 1924. The oak symbolizes steadfastness, strength and loyalty.

Army Regulations established the eligibility requirements for the award. During the World War II and Korean War years, the award could be earned by soldiers below the rank of Colonel serving with an infantry or special forces military occupational specialty who have satisfactorily performed duty while assigned as a member of an infantry or special forces unit when the unit was engaged in active ground combat.

Specific criteria for later wars have been established. The primary requirement—that a soldier must be assigned to an infantry unit during such time as the unit is engaged in active ground combat—remained in effect.

In developing the CIB, the War Department did not ignore the contributions of other branches of service. Their contributions to the overall war effort were certainly noted, but the War Department decided that other awards and decorations were sufficient to recognize the contributions by those who served in other branches.


Company C, as part of the 180th Infantry Regimental Combat Team (RCT), consisting of the regiment with supporting artillery units, entered combat in Korea on December 5, 1951, temporarily attached to the 1st Cavalry Division while the two divisions were exchanging assignments—with the Cavalry units moving to Hokkaido, Japan, to assume the defensive assignment in that northernmost of the Japanese islands. All elements of the 45th Division did not arrive in Korea until the end of December.

The 180th Infantry Regiment began replacing the 5th Cavalry Regiment, assuming responsibility for a sector of an emerging Main Line of Resistance (MLR) along "Line Jamestown." As 1951 ended, all elements of the 45th Division were in Korea in a combat status and the 179th Infantry Regiment joined the 180th Infantry Regiment along the front lines, with the Ninth Republic of Korea (ROK) Division to the right of the 180th Infantry Regiment and with the U. S. 3d Infantry Division on the left flank of the 179th Infantry Regiment. The 279th Infantry Regiment was in a division reserve position.

In mid-January 1952, the 279th Infantry Regiment relieved the 180th Infantry Regiment, and Company C, along with the balance of the regiment, reverted to the division reserve assignment.

During the weeks of December and January, Company C platoons and those from other companies along the front were involved in a series of ambush and reconnaissance patrols against strong enemy positions in the sector.

Despite bitter resistance by the Chinese and North Korean forces, the 180th's combat units were successful and inflicted heavy casualties upon the enemy. The 180th Infantry Regiment's troops did not go unscathed in those battles. Division records indicate that the Regiment's battle casualties for the month totaled 156 soldiers wounded or killed.

Throughout those days, the supporting artillery units placed heavy artillery fire on known and suspected enemy positions and personnel in the area.


The families back home often did not know of the day-by-day life of the hometown soldiers who were in far-off Korea fighting a war. As is true in all wars, the daily routine, memorable to those who lived it, went largely untold.

From time to time, I wanted the families in Ada to be aware of some of the activities of their sons, fathers, brothers and uncles who were "with the Thunderbirds" in Korea.

During the 45th Infantry Division's months of service in Japan and Korea, I served as an unofficial "war correspondent" for Company C's hometown newspaper, *The Ada Evening News*, the daily newspaper published in Ada, Oklahoma. Articles were prepared on a regular basis and mailed to the newspaper, as time and events permitted.

Some, but not all, these stories were told.


The first awarding of Combat Infantryman Badges to the qualifying soldiers of Company C came in February 1952 during a company size formation held in a safe valley area in the shadows of the snow-covered hills and mountains of North Korea. The beautiful blue and silver badges were handed to individual soldiers by Captain Garnett E.

Mercer, Company C's commanding officer. Each man was called to the front of the assembled troops as I stood next to Captain Mercer to read their names from the Special Order that authorized the awards and cited each of the qualifying soldiers.

Company C's soldiers had been involved in front-line combat service for approximately five weeks when the unit was first relieved and reassigned to a reserve position.

Citations for the individual soldiers who were awarded the Combat Infantryman Badge included language to commend them for performance in "ground combat action . . . having been personally present and under hostile enemy fire while serving with Company C, 180th Infantry Regiment, in the Yon'chon-Ch'orwon sector of North Korea, during the period of 5 December 1951 to 15 January 1952."

Over the years the military has developed a pyramid of honors, a listing of awards, medals and decorations for its members, in an effort to recognize the G.I. for a job well done, service rendered, and for valor. Without a doubt, among all those honors, the Combat Infantryman Badge is the infantryman's most prestigious award—next to the Medal of Honor.

There would be other such ceremonies in future months to honor soldiers of Company C and other units for their combat service. Each of us who received the CIB would treasure the award for the remainder or our lives— and cherish as brothers the men with whom we served during those days of war in Korea.

# Combat Infantryman's Badge Awarded to Many in Co. C

## More Than 200 From Unit in 180th Inf. Reg. Rec In Ceremony in Shadows of Korea's Battle Scarr

**By M/Sgt. Clarence G. Oliver, Jr.**

During a company sized formation, held recently in the shadows of Korea's battle scarred hills, the award of the Combat Infantryman's Badge was made to over two hundred members of Company C, 180th Infantry Regiment.

The award, a blue and silver badge, one of the most prized possessions of an infantry soldier in the United States Army, was awarded to the members of that unit for their performance of duty in recent combat action against the enemy forces in Korea.

...entation was made individ... ...ier by Captain ...Vir-

award, having rece award while servi men during Worl men are Capt. C War, W. Va.: ; Kiker, Childre George F. M Penn.: Sfc. Oklahoma: thews, Tv Pfc. Benj Kentucky Memb saw ac Decem of the Comb the 'air ticle soldiers flurries of the 45 well as the wors hind them.

# Co. C Back At Front After Rest

## Men Keep Busy, Many of Them Keenly Interested I 'Phase Out' Return

**By M-Sgt. CLARENCE OLIVER**

Snow-covered hills are still the common sight in this western sector of Korea where Company C, of the 180th Infantry is presently located, but a pre-spring warmth is in the air and the Thunderbird soldiers welcome it. Although snow flurries are still frequent, members of the 45th Infantry Division, as well as all soldiers in Korea, have the worst of the Korean winter behind them.

The mountains that were heavily covered with snow only a few days ago have now become spotted with patches of brown, indicating that a warmer, but much wetter lies ahead.

# Ada Soldiers Among Minded Thunderbird

**M SGT. CLARENCE G OLIVER, J**

CAMP MONTE STRONG, Ja-n— (Special) —Sports minded underbirds turned their eyes ward athletic activities thi ck as a Division controlled letic program got underway in big fashion.

Baseball has taken the spot-ht for the present time, but actice is already underway for Division football team that asts several college and high-tool all star names on the line

Ada's sports fan probably re-mber big Joe W. Dunham who ched several games for Ada ghschool, played ball with the American Legion Juniors and er made his bid in semi-pro th a Dalhart, Texas, team. Dun-m, now Sergeant First Class nham in Company C. 180th antry, has found his berth on 180th Regimental Combat m nine

### Dunham Saves Game

Last week he brought a gam of the fire when he went ring the sixth inning to br team from behind for a over the 179th Regimen mbat team baseballers.

guard lin on the 18 good pre do not o averages

this area from headquarters in Thunderbird soldiers indicate that ed from the future

*Receiving the Combat Infantryman Badge (CIB) was a major honor. First awards to Company C soldiers were presented in February 1952. The first person to receive the award from Company Commander Captain Garnet E. Mercer (center) was First Lieutenant W. Kiker of Childress, Texas. Both Kiker and Mercer received their second CIBs, after having received that honor during World War II service in Europe. Master Sergeant Clarence G. Oliver, Jr., unit administrative officer, reads the award orders.*

*Sergeant First Class Stanley D. Walker of Ada, Oklahoma, receives a CIB from Captain Garnet E.Mercer.*

*(February 1952)*

*Snow, ice and below zero weather created difficult conditions in the battle areas of North Korea. Sergeant First Class Benny C. Floyd of Ada, Oklahoma, leads a squad from Company C along a snow-covered road in an area west of Ch'orwon, North Korea, shortly after the 180th Infantry Regimental Combat Team replaced troops of the 1st Cavalry Division in December 1951. On the right is a burned out enemy truck, destroyed by 1st Cavalry Division units during earlier fighting with Chinese troops for control of the area*

*(45th Division News Photo by Pfc. Jack Gunter)*
*(December 1951)*

**COMBAT INFANTRYMAN BADGE**

ESTABLISHED BY THE SECRETARY OF WAR
AS ANNOUNCED IN WAR DEPARTMENT CIRCULAR 269

TO ALL THOSE WHO SEE THESE PRESENTS GREETING

GIVEN UNDER

ON

## Combat Infantryman Badge Goes to 23 Ada Thunderbirds

WITH THE 45TH DIVISION IN KOREA — Twenty-three men from Ada, Okla., recently were awarded the Combat Infantry Badge, symbol of close-quarter fighting with the enemy, while serving with the 45th Infantry Division in Korea.

The men, all members of Company C, 180th Infantry Regiment, are: M/Sgt. Kenneth R. Bunch, son of Mr. and Mrs. John J. Bunch, 803 South Stockton, a platoon sergeant.

First Lt. Donald T. Clark, son of Mr. and Mrs. Bill Clark and husband of Mrs. Anna Lou Clark, 931 East Fifth, a platoon leader.

M/Sgt. Harold G. Evans, son of Mr. and Mrs. Harry Evans, 514 West 15th, first sergeant.

Sergeant First Class Ben G. Floyd, son of Mr. and Mrs. Haskell Floyd, 115 West 22nd, a squad leader.

Sergeant First Class Walter J. Gray, son of Mr. and Mrs. W. C. Gray of Route 3, and husband of Mrs. Bobbie Gray, 226 West 18th, a squad leader.

Sgt. Billie Lewis Gray, whose wife, Ginger, and parents, Mr. and Mrs. W. C. Gray, live on Route 3, a squad leader.

Sergeant First Class Jack Hohbird, whose father, P. M. Hohbird, lives in Charleston, S. C., and

Virginia, lives on Route 4, and whose parents, Mr. and Mrs. Otis Jones, live at 620 West 15th, an assistant squad leader.

Sgt. James A. Kimbey, son of Mr. and Mrs. H. L. Kimbey, 706 West Tenth, a cook.

Sergeant First Class Charles McGuire, son of Mr. and Mrs. Joe McGuire, 518 North Francis, a mortar section leader.

Cpl. David F. Morgan, son of Mrs. May E. Morgan (father deceased) of Route 1, a squad leader.

Cpl. Charles R. Morgan, son of Mrs. May Morgan of Route 1, a machine gunner.

Pfc. William D. Mullins, 216 West 12th, a rifleman.

M/Sgt. Clarence G. Oliver Jr., whose wife, Vinita, lives at 326 West Fourth, and whose parents, live at 521 West Sixth, a unit administrator.

Sergeant First Class Bobby A. Roberts, son of Mr. and Mrs. J. F. Roberts, 1023 North Ash, a squad leader.

Cpl. Bobby G. Scott, son of Mrs. Ethel Scott (father deceased), 417 East Eighth, a squad leader.

Sergeant First Class Paul M. Scott, son of Mr. and Mrs. Walter P. Scott, 436 East Ninth, a supply sergeant (second award).

Pfc. Jim See, son of Mr. and Mrs. L. A. See, 709 West Fifth, an munition bearer.

Sgt. Melvin L. Taylor, whose wife, Jackie, and parents, Mr. and Mrs. W. F. Taylor, live at 230 West 15th, a squad leader.

Sergeant First Class Kenneth H. ... son of Mr. and Mrs. John P.

*The Ada Evening News, Company C's hometown newspaper, reported on the awarding of Combat Infantryman Badges to soldiers in a page one article that appeared in the March 24, 1952, edition of the newspaper.*
*Archives, The Ada Evening News*
*Ada, Oklahoma*

133

*Sergeant First Class Gerald West of Ada, Oklahoma, assistant platoon sergeant, shows the stress and exhaustion of battle after leading an attack on Chinese positions near Pork Chop Hill. During the attack, a Chinese hand grenade landed at his feet, but failed to explode. The experience left him emotionally drained.*

*A week later, West was wounded during a Chinese attack on an outpost. He was awarded a Purple Heart.*

*(February 1952)*

## SFC Gerald West Has Purple Heart

### Adan Hospitalized by Grenade Fragments, Now Back at Front

SFC Gerald L. West, son of Mr. and Mrs. Gerald West 418½ South Mississippi, has been awarded a Purple Heart for injuries received in Korea fighting, according to information received by his parents.

A member of Company C, 180th Infantry, Sgt. West was serving with an outpost patrol when an enemy threw a hand grenade in his direction.

The Ada sergeant attempted to get out of the way, but fragments hit him in the hand.

He was placed in a hospital for several days, but has already returned to action.

Serving as assistant platoon leader, SFC West was operating from headquarters that had been set up near Saman-gol, North Korea.

The incident took place Wednesday, February 20, and kept him out of action about three weeks, according to information received by his parents.

# Chapter Ten

## Rescue of Wounded Warrior—

One of my best childhood friends living in the neighborhood where I was "born and raised," as people in my hometown of Ada, Oklahoma, would say, was Ben Floyd. The neighborhood of our youth was in an older part of the city and encircled the Irving Grade School grounds.

Ben's family, at that time, lived in a house on West Fourth Street, directly across the street north of Irving Grade School, just two blocks north of my home. The family later moved to another house in the same neighborhood, one block south of my home.

Ben was a year or so younger that I, but that minor age difference didn't matter with boys—especially the small group in our neighborhood. He had a younger brother, Joe Mac, two years younger than Ben.

The three of us became good friends during the elementary school years. This was a friendship that was to continue into adulthood.

Ben and Joe Mac often invited me to their home after school, on weekends and during summer days. Many of those days were spent on the school grounds across the street. Usually, though, since several trees shaded the Floyd's yard, both front and back, the playtime was enjoyed under—and up in—the trees in the Floyd's front yard.

Ben and Joe Mac enlisted in the hometown National Guard unit, Company C, just as soon as they approached the end of their senior years in high school. Both "stretched the truth" a bit about their ages—just as had several others of us in the unit—claiming to be the mandatory 18 years of age required for enlisting. Their parents had reluctantly agreed to the boys enlisting in the unit. Many of their friends were already "in the Guard," and Ben and Joe Mac joined up.

Both were good soldiers, learned quickly, and assumed leadership responsibilities. When Company C arrived in Korea, the Floyd brothers were already non-commissioned officers—Ben, a Sergeant First Class, assistant platoon sergeant; and Joe, a Sergeant, rifle squad leader.

The brothers were in Company C's second platoon, one of the best-performing platoons in the unit.

There was some concern in the nation—and in Ada, Oklahoma—about close relatives serving together in the same unit in a combat zone.

Following the tragic loss of the five Sullivan brothers—George Thomas, Francis Henry, Joseph Eugene, Madison Abel, and Albert Leo—of Waterloo, Iowa, when the Navy light cruiser, the *U.S.S. Juneau*, was sunk by a torpedo from a Japanese submarine in an intense naval battle near Guadalcanal on November 13, 1942, the nation grieved with that family over such a loss. Political and military leaders wanted to avoid similar losses in the future.

The United States Congress, from time to time, had considered legislation that would restrict assignment of relatives in combat. An amended section of the Military Selective Service Act did provide that "no man may be drafted, unless he volunteers for induction, if he is considered to be the sole surviving son" under various criteria that was set up to determine such status. But, that applied to "being drafted," and did not pertain to limitations on voluntary service or unit assignment.

Nevertheless, the concern was still expressed about members of the same family serving together in combat.

Waterloo, Iowa, the hometown of the Sullivan family, was a community of fewer than 50,000 people in 1942 when the five Sullivan brothers died together. The entire community was devastated with that loss of life in one family.

Ada, Oklahoma, the home community of Company C, was a much smaller community than Waterloo, Iowa. There were about 15,000 people living in Ada. Since Company C was a hometown unit, a number of those who enlisted were related. At the time of the unit's call to active duty just a few weeks after the beginning of the Korean War, there were at least four sets of brothers serving together in Company C, along with many cousins, uncles, brothers-in-law and other more distant relatives.

The number of sets of brothers was reduced slightly by transfers, but when Company C was preparing to deploy to Korea, three sets of brothers—including Ben and Joe Mac Floyd— remained in the unit.

In Hokkaido, Japan, after the unit completed every phase of training, military commanders wanted to separate the brothers. Ben and Joe Mac Floyd were approached with the suggestion that the younger brother, Joe Mac, be transferred to Headquarters Company.

Joe Mac remembered that he strongly objected to leaving the rifle platoon assignment where he had become a rifle squad leader and where his brother, Ben, was an assistant platoon sergeant. Someone wanted to separate the brothers. The brothers didn't like that idea.

The other members of the platoon and Joe Mac's squad had trained as a unit for months, and they wanted to remain together. They trusted each other. Such trust is important in combat.

"I did not think that I should be transferred just when we were about to move into a real combat situation," Joe Mac remembered.

Since regulations did not require such separation, the brothers were permitted to remain together.

In later years, Joe Mac often thought, "If I had transferred to Headquarters Company, I probably would not have been wounded in Korea and my life may have been somewhat different."

Wisely, he added, "But who knows?"


Officers in high places most certainly were provided official notice that the 45th Infantry Division was headed to Korea, but the formal notice didn't seem to get down the line to men in the units. Most of us suspected that deployment to Korea was imminent.

None of us remembers receiving the official word that advised us, "Men you are going to Korea."

Things just started to happen.

Instructions came for each squad leader to check that all men in the unit had current identification tags— "dog tags," as most of us referred to the small tags that were hanging around our necks—and to make certain that those wearing glasses had two pairs.

Then, supply sergeants began issuing to each member of the unit the new down-filled sleeping bags, parkas, pile caps, and shoepac boots.

It didn't take a genius to know what was taking place.

The rumors were there. The Japanese shopkeepers and the girls in the numerous bars in the nearby city of Chitose seemed to know that the 45th Infantry Division was leaving for Korea.

So much for security of military operations!

A USO type group came to Camp Chitose to entertain the troops with the typical program of music, jokes and attractive girls. It was a good show.

For the finale, the entire cast sang a song about "burp guns and mortars and some high, high mountains."

"That clarified our destination." Sergeant Floyd recalled.

A few days before the unit was to depart Hokkaido for "points unknown," that northernmost island of Japan was covered with heavy snow. Almost overnight, the snow was knee-deep, with drifts up to several feet deep.

When Company C "fell out" to leave for the port to board a ship, the troopers carried rifles, wore steel helmets, parkas, full field packs with horseshoe roll, weapons and laundry-duffle bags filled with all other belongings.

Joe Mac wrote about the march to the nearby railroad depot to board the train and remembered the "march" with these thoughts, "It was impossible to get the laundry bag on our shoulders because of the horseshoe roll on the packs, and we ended up dragging the bag."

He said he felt that the march-walk to the railroad depot "was the sloppiest, most disorganized movement we had ever made."


Company C, along with other units that formed the 180th Infantry Regimental Combat Team, landed in Korea at Inch' on and almost immediately moved toward the front to begin relieving elements of the 1st Cavalry Division.

This was the Christmas season—but one vastly different than was being observed back home where people were buying gifts, mailing greeting cards, decorating Christmas trees and homes. The thoughts of the men of Company C were on much more immediate matters related to war.

Despite their being in a combat zone, December was a special month for Ben and Joe Mac Floyd. Both brothers celebrated birthdays during that month—Joe Mac on December 6 and Ben on December 7. From a gift-receiving standpoint, having birthdays just a few days before Christmas may have cut into the number of gifts the boys received on Christmas morning during their childhood years.

They were no longer "boys." Ben was 21 and Joe Mac was 19. They had other concerns during the Christmas season in 1951.

After landing at Inch' on and traveling by train to a railroad junction near Uijongbu and a truck convey on north, Company C spent a brief period in a rear area while plans were made for the unit to replace 1st Cavalry Division troops who were deployed in the front line positions.

Some mail from family members—letters and packages originally headed to Japan—had been diverted to Korea and arrived while the unit was in the area making preparations for movement to the front. There was a package addressed to both the Floyd brothers—Ben and Joe Mac. It was a birthday cake from home, packed in popcorn for a cushioning effect. Surprisingly, the cake was intact. Their birthdays were celebrated with their Second Platoon buddies—and a few others who could "mooch" a piece of home-baked birthday cake.

There weren't any birthday cake candles, but some friends, although off key at times, sang the "Happy Birthday" melody, with sincerity. The birthday party was a joyous occasion for Ben and Joe Mac Floyd and friends. All of us were 10,000 miles from home.

None of us knew what was ahead during these days before Christmas 1951. The lives of the two brothers would be changed in an instant just a few days later on December 20—a day neither would ever forget.

Final preparations were made for the movement to the front. Commanders made a decision that the replacement of 1st Cavalry Division front line troops by Company C and other units of the 180th Infantry Regimental Combat Team would be a "nighttime relief in place" action.

Relieving a unit in place in combat can be a bit challenging in its own right. Doing so at night is significantly more difficult. Secrecy was important in order to prevent the enemy from knowing that new troops were occupying the positions. Such knowledge by the enemy could encourage an attack on new troops in unfamiliar territory.

Company officers and selected noncommissioned officers made carefully coordinated daytime visits to the forward positions in order to become familiar with the area, the battle line positions, location of bunkers, automatic weapons, outposts and other important sites.

When the nighttime replacement of troops began, the soldiers of Company C would arrive at a bunker, observation post, a foxhole or other position, tap on the shoulder of a soldier in place, whisper to him, and move in to take over the position.


The nighttime relief operations plan called for not only taking over positions but also accepting the crew-served weapons, some other heavy equipment and vehicles of the Cavalry unit.

The advantage of taking control of the machineguns, mortars, bazookas and the recoilless rifles was that the weapons were already in place in defensive positions, the weapons were "zeroed in" for accuracy of fire at strategic points, and the zones of fire. Those zones were marked on maps and stakes in the ground indicated some. That takes time. By accepting the weapons in place, our unit would be immediately able to defend a position should an enemy attack occur.

Good strategy—normally.


The terrain of the Korean peninsula north of the 38th parallel where troops of the 180th Infantry Regiment moved into position was dominated by steep-sided hills that overlooked narrow valleys, some wide enough for only a stream or a narrow road. In some areas, there were rice paddies that had once been farmed, but now were abandoned. Ruins of small villages and isolated houses were in the area.

Most of Company C was deployed along the snow-covered range that overlooked part of the Yokkuk-ch'on River valley, where the river meandered between steep hills. The unit also had responsibility for a wide, flat area in the valley. One rifle platoon held outposts in that exposed and vulnerable valley and linked on the right flank with a company from a Republic of Korea (ROK) division.

To most of us from Oklahoma, the rugged, steep hills were considered "mountains," although their actual height, the elevation above sea level, seemed to require that they be designated as "hills."

These front line positions were only recently established.

The historic 1st Cavalry Division had been involved in battles in Korea since storming ashore near Pusan on the southern tip of the peninsula in July 1950 to relieve elements of the 24th Infantry Division. During the year that followed, the division, along with other Eighth Army units, battled the North Korean and Chinese armies in the "see-saw" fighting throughout the country.

Just weeks before the 180th Infantry Regimental Combat Team arrived in Korea, the Cavalry units repulsed waves of Red Chinese with hand-to-hand combat and then attacked Chinese positions south of the Yokkuk-ch'on River.

During October and November, hills were taken, lost and retaken.

Those Cavalry troops recaptured the strategic Hill 418 on which the northern end of the Jamestown Line became anchored. After repulsing Chinese counterattacks, the Cavalry units took possession of Hill 272 and "Old Baldy," critical terrain on the Jamestown Line.

Company C and other elements of the 180th Infantry Regimental Combat Team were to move into those positions along the Jamestown Line.

Chinese Army units occupied positions on higher hills north and northwest of the valley,

The ruins of the demolished city of Ch'orwan, North Korea, could be seen in the distance, about four miles to the east of our positions. Across the valley to the northeast was the strategic Whitehorse Mountain, held by the Chinese. Directly to the north was a pointed ridge that extended south into the valley. That ridge was on the north side of the river and was occupied, for the moment, by our unit.

That oddly shaped pointed ridge was given the name of "Arrowhead" because when viewed on a map, the unique shape of the terrain very much resembled a flint arrowhead that Indians used on the tips of hunting arrow.

We Oklahomans knew about such things.

Just to the west was another strategic hill that became known as "T-Bone Hill," so named because the hill's contours on the military map resembled a T-bone steak, at least for those with a bit of imagination.

Dozens of "no-name" hills that had been fought for, won, lost, won again and probably would be military objectives in the days to come were on both sides of the river.

The entire area was blanketed in snow, the temperature was in the below-zero range, and for the moment, the river that ran between our positions and the enemy's positions was ice covered.


The sound strategy of accepting the crew-served weapons in place from the unit being relieved would insure that Company C and similar units in the battalion would be immediately able to defend a position should an enemy attack occur.

A concern of our troops, though, was a question about whether all the crew-served weapons had been properly maintained and were fully operational. Also, some weapons have their own peculiarities that individual soldiers soon learn and know how to correct or accommodate.

How long would it take to learn about those weapons?

The vehicles and equipment our unit left in Hokkaido were in good condition. Some of the vehicles and weapons that our unit received now were hardly in that category.

Units of the 1st Cavalry Division had been in several hard-fought battles in North Korea just weeks before our 180th Infantry Regimental Combat Team began this phase-in replacement. The "Jamestown Line" that now marked the main line of resistance (MLR) was established in October 1951, just two months earlier and the vehicles, weapons and heavy equipment that were being inherited from the 1st Cavalry Division were "war-weary."

Some needed to be replaced—a process that can be easier said than done. Requesting and obtaining a new replacement for a malfunctioning crew-served weapon didn't happen overnight.

An example of the status of some of the equipment was one 30-caliber machinegun that had been left "in place" and turned over to the Second Platoon's weapons squad.

Shortly after moving into the new positions, gunners were directed to do a "weapons check" on each crew-served weapon. Sergeant Joe Mac Floyd recalled that the machine gun placed near his squad's position didn't fire properly.

He said, "The Cav's light 30-caliber machinegun was a 'single shot.' It would fire one round and the gunner would have to manually eject the shell case."

That was a concern to the rifle squads that depended on the supporting fire from the machineguns manned by the platoon's fourth squad, the weapons squad.

The Army's 30-caliber M-1919 A-4 Light Machine Gun (LMG) was a critical weapon for an Infantry rifle company. This 41-pound machinegun, with tripod mount, was capable of sustained fire at 400-550 rounds per minute, with cartridges fed from a 250-round belt of ammunition. The machine gun had an effective range of 1,100 yards. The weapon used the same cartridge as the M-1 Garand rifle and the Browning Automatic Rifle (BAR), the other basic weapons for the rifle squads.

This was an infantry platoon's machinegun—critical in both attack and defensive operations.

The malfunctioning machinegun that had just been inherited by Company C was less effective than another rifle.

Sergeant Floyd began to wonder how long it would take to repair or replace that critical weapon.

He would never learn the answer to that question.

December 20, 1951, was just another cold winter day on the front lines in Korea for the soldiers of Company C. The ground was frozen solid and covered in snow. The wind had abated a bit and the temperature hovered a few degrees below the freezing point. Some soldiers were able to remove the heavy and cumbersome arctic parkas in favor of wearing insulated field jackets as they made improvements to their defensive positions.

For Sergeant Joe Mac Floyd, this was to be a day that would change his life forever. He became Company C's first casualty of the Korean War. His rescue and survival are considered by many of his peers as miraculous.

Reflecting on the day a half-century later, Sergeant Floyd said that he didn't remember exactly what the unit was doing that day. His rifle squad had been instructed to "check the wire in front of our positions."

His squad was deployed on the forward slope of a steep hill that overlooked the Yokkuk-ch'on River valley. Located in front of the positions, lower on the hill toward the valley area, were defensive barriers of barbed wire, trip flares and other devices to warn of an enemy intrusion into the area, to snare approaching enemy soldiers and to disrupt any enemy attack on the Company's positions.

The main defense positions for the rifle squads were gun pits and foxholes strung along the forward slope near the top of the hill and along flanking ridges. Supporting bunkers were near the top of the hills.

Military barbed wire, often with empty C-ration tin cans tied to the wire as additional warning devices, is a very effective barrier that can slow enemy troop movements. With razor sharp barbs, the coiled wire designed for military use is more vicious in nature than regular stockman's wire used to fence farms and ranch land. One or two rows of coiled barbed concertina wire entanglements make formidable obstacles for attacking troops.

Trip flares, booby traps and sometimes anti-personnel mines usually are placed in front of the barbed wire to warn defenders and to maim or kill attackers.

A trip flare is a small ground flare that is triggered by a wire that is strung at ground level across a possible attack route so the flare is ignited when an enemy soldier moving toward the defensive position trips the wire. When "tripped," a magnesium flare is shot straight up. The flare burns for 90 seconds.

Sergeant Joe Mac Floyd encountered such a flare as he crawled over and under barbed wire and walked along the barrier to check the condition of the wire and warning devices.

Some of the wire, flares and other devices had been put in place by the former Cavalry unit troopers. Company C soldiers examined the terrain for existing flare and booby trap locations and added to or improved the defensive positions after relieving the former unit.

Sergeant Floyd's foot struck a hidden trip wire. The connected flare leaped into the air and exploding metal fragments ripped into Sergeant Floyd's head, arm and hand. Part of his forehead was severely damaged and a skull area was shattered. He fell to the ground, a severely wounded Infantryman.

One of our "warriors" was down!

Nearby rifle squad members rushed to the wounded Sergeant Floyd, calling for the medic assigned to the platoon.

The combat medic who was assigned to the platoon from Medical Company, 180th Infantry Regiment, crawled through the barbed wire barrier, dragging his medical aid kit and a collapsible light metal and canvas litter stretcher that could be used in a rescue effort. He began administering emergency care to Sergeant Floyd who clearly was in critical condition. That he would survive the injuries was in

147

great doubt in the minds of the medic and others who saw the massive head injuries.

The blast of the exploding trip flare caused great damage to the heavy steel helmet that Sergeant Floyd was wearing. The helmet had diverted part of the blast. Without that protection, though, the entire top of Sergeant Floyd's head most likely would have been shattered by the flying metal and burning magnesium.

Writing about that day more than five decades later, Sergeant Floyd recalled, "I remember the weather had moderated the day I was injured. I was wearing my field jacket and steel helmet instead of the usual dress of parka and soft pile cap. All the troops grumbled about having to wear the steel helmet during training, but that steel pot saved my life."

Details of the explosion, of being wounded and of the rescue effort are blank spots in Joe Mac's memories of the day. His next memories of that time are from days later in a hospital near Seoul.

The soldiers around him, though, have vivid memories of the incident and the challenging rescue effort that required men to reach deep within themselves for strength and energy in a team effort to save a wounded friend.

Corporal Kemper W. Chambers, then of Rockaway, New Jersey, was a rifleman in the squad, and Sergeant First Class Joe Hill Floyd of Ada, Oklahoma, a squad leader, were among those who helped in the rescue effort. Both recalled that Joe Mac's brother, Sergeant First Class Ben C. Floyd "was the first" to reach the injured soldier and was frantic in seeking assistance. Combat Medic Duane M. Laws of Mexico, New York, a member of Medical Company, 180th Infantry Regiment, who was assigned to the second squad, rushed to the injured soldier.

The wounded Joe Mac Floyd lay in the snow near the base of the hill, forward of the barbed wire barrier, clearly in view of enemy soldiers who occupied the hills across the valley. Getting Joe Mac to a location behind the front lines in order to obtain medical assistance other than the emergency care of the platoon medic would require climbing up the steep hill through ice, snow, scrub trees, brush, rocks— as well as getting the injured soldier over, under or through the barbed wire barrier strung across in front of the unit's positions.

The climb to the top of the hill required mountain-climbing skills, using hands and feet to pull and push up the almost 60-degree slope. Doing so with a rifle strung across the shoulder or carrying other fighting equipment was difficult in itself.

How could that climb be accomplished while trying to carry a wounded soldier?

Corporal Chambers recalled that "all of the platoon helped" in the Herculean effort of getting the litter on which the almost lifeless Joe Mac lay "up the hill and down the other side" to a path that led toward to an area where a Jeep could be driven to become an emergency ambulance.[10]

The ingenious platoon members formed a human chain of at least 12 soldiers, linked hand-to-hand to drag and carry the stretcher and the injured Sergeant Floyd up the hill and down the other side. The rescuers at times were literally clawing their way in the ice and snow.

Sergeant First Class Joe Hill Floyd recalled that a very difficult part of the rescue effort was that of "getting through the barbed wire" barrier. Once that was accomplished, the climb was one of overcoming the steep terrain and the frozen snow and ice. The chain of soldiers inched

---

[10] Chambers, Kemper W. Personal correspondence to author, October 23, 2006.

upward to the top and inched downward on the other side in reverse of the climb.[11]

Six members of the "chain" were in front of the stretcher on which the unconscious Joe Mac lay. The combat medic Duane Laws was in the lead position on the right side of the stretcher, giving constant attention and aid. Sergeant First Class Ben C. Floyd, the injured soldier's brother, was on the left side of the stretcher. The remainder of the "chain" was behind the stretcher, pushing the stretcher and others up the hill. Once the top of the hill was reached, the hand-to-hand chain was continued, but now became one of trying to avoid a fast slide down the steep reverse slope.

Everyone in the chain was exhausted long before the top was reached. Somehow, they found the strength and energy to continue. The climb up and the slippery trip down the reverse slope required about five hours.

Under most conditions, with such severe injuries, Joe Mac would have died during such a time-consuming rescue. Despite the pressure bandages the medic placed on his head, Joe Mac might have bled to death but for the severe cold weather. The freezing temperature slowed the bleeding.

The rescue effort was similar to recovering an injured or dead mountain climber—but without the specialized ropes, pulleys and other equipment available for those rescue efforts.

Finally, at the bottom of the hill, the exhausted team of soldiers carried the stretcher—and Joe Mac—down a path to an area that one of Company C's Jeeps could reach. The stretcher was placed across the hood of the Jeep, and the wounded soldier was driven as quickly as safety permitted over a narrow, snow-packed trail to the battalion medical aid station.

---

[11] Hill, Joe Hill. Personal correspondence to author, January 2005

More than six hours had passed since Joe Mac had been wounded.

The doctor and medic who staffed the battalion aid station bunker quickly administered the first of any advanced emergency care beyond that given by the combat medic in order to stabilize the wounded soldier and prepare him for evacuation by ambulance to the Mobile Army Surgical Hospital (MASH) unit, located a few miles further south of the front line positions.

Somehow—almost certainly by God's hand—Joe Mac survived the many hours of being dragged, pulled and carried up and down a mountain and a rough ride while strapped across the hood of a Jeep to reach the MASH unit where surgeons could begin removing shattered bone from his skull, attempt to prevent further damage to his exposed brain, and proceed with other life-saving medical care.

He was unconscious most of that time.


An Associated Press photographer captured on film the valiant action of the soldiers linked hand-to-hand in the rescue effort in a news photograph taken of the rescuers struggling in the snow as they approached the top of the hill. The photograph was printed in a few newspapers across the United States, but without identifying any of the people who were involved in the heroic action.

Surprisingly, the photograph apparently did not appear in a major Oklahoma newspaper.

A newspaper clipping of the photograph from the January 5, 1952, issue of the *Star-Ledger*, a daily newspaper published in Newark, New Jersey, was saved by a relative and found its way to the family of Joe Hill Floyd, one of the men in the photograph. The photo caption in the New Jersey newspaper simply explained, "Men of the 45th Infantry Division form a human chain to help get up a snowy Korean hill as they carry one of their wounded men back to their position."

More than 50 years later, after extensive research, Kevin O'Sullivan of the Associated Press office staff in New York City, New York, responded to my request and coordinated a search to find the original negative in the AP achieves. He was successful. The AP staff provided a new photograph and authorized reproduction of the news photograph for this book.

Through the diligent effort of Joe Hill Floyd and Kemper W. Chambers, who participated in the rescue effort, the identification of several, not all, of the soldiers who participated in this effort has been established.

Among those in the human chain of rescuers were Sergeant First Class Joe Dunham; Sergeant First Class Joe Hill Floyd, a cousin of the wounded soldier; Sergeant First Class Benny C. Floyd, the injured soldier's brother, all of Ada, Oklahoma; Private First Class Earl J. Lebouf, Theriot, Louisiana; Corporal Robert D. Fitzjerrell, North Little Rock, Arkansas; Private First Class Nolan N. Blount, Albany, Louisiana; Corporal Edward J. Bankos, Boonton, New Jersey; Private First Class Pablo Velasquez, Price, Utah; Private First Class Edgar L. Schmidt, Milwaukee, Wisconsin; and Corporal Kemper W. Chambers, Rockaway, New Jersey.

The valiant combat medic who provided the life-saving first medical assistance was Private First Class Duane M. Laws, Mexico, New York. Among the medics from Medical Company, 180th Infantry Regiment, who were attached to Company C's second platoon during that time were Private First Class Bill Burnett, Washington, D.C., and Private First Class Arthur M. Walker, Toccoa, Georgia, who later was awarded the Silver Star for heroic battlefield rescue effort two months later near the base of Pork Chop Hill.

These combat medics—and the fellow soldiers who linked hand-to-hand to save Joe Mac Floyd—served with great honor that day.

Among my administrative responsibilities for Company C was the early morning preparation of the U. S. Army Daily Morning Report, a small document created each morning, as the name implies, to record events of the previous 24 hours. The reports prepared in Korea were in duplicate on a narrow form with very limited space for entries and reflected the unit's strength that day and information about those individuals who were not "present and accounted for" that day. The report listed promotions or demotion, persons who were killed (KIA), wounded (WIA) or missing in action (MIA). The reports also indicated the individuals who were being assigned to the unit, leaving the unit, going to a hospital for treatment, or another activity for training.

Among the information that I typed on the Daily Morning Report to reflect action of December 20, 1951, was a short entry that contained only this basic information:

*Floyd, Joe M., Sgt., seriously WIA from missile.*
*Evacuated to 121ˢᵗ Evacuation Hospital,*
*Yongdungp'o, South Korea.*

There is much more to the story.

I made a daily effort through contacts at battalion, regimental and division levels to trace Joe Mac's location in order to advise his brother and friends of his status. He remained at the 121ˢᵗ Evacuation Hospital for several days. His medical status remained "serious." But, he was alive, being treated, and was being prepared for transfer to Japan and then back to the United States.

Most of us knew that this was the end of the Army career for Sergeant Joe Mac Floyd. At age 19 and a few days, he was "headed home." He would get there, though, only after months of surgery and therapy.

### Sergeant Joe M. Floyd Reflects—[12]

Sergeant Joe Mac Floyd woke up—but in a bit of a daze.

He was confused, unsure of what had happened to him and a bit baffled about his location. He quickly determined that he was in some kind of medical facility, that he had a cast on one hand and that his head was hurting.

Joe Mac recalled that he did not have any idea of how many hours, or even days, had passed since he had crossed the barbed wire barrier in front of Company C's positions to "check the wire." He knew nothing about the explosion that erupted when his foot tripped over that fateful wire in the snow. His memory of the time and incidents between then and his present situation—the blast, the injury, and all that followed—was completely blank.

"The medical personnel told me I had suffered an injury to my head and left hand," Joe Mac said as he recalled the events that began to unfold. He saw that his left hand was in a cast.

Joe Mac remembered that he thought, "I would be returned to my unit when the injuries healed."

A return to the unit was not in his future.

He soon learned that he was being "evacuated" from Korea and that he was at that moment in the U.S. Army's 121st Evacuation Hospital.

The 121st Evacuation Hospital was a 400-bed hospital that had been established in a converted school building in Yongdungp'o, near Seoul, South Korea.

---

[12] Floyd, Joe Mac, Personal Correspondence to author, 2006.

Sergeant Floyd, in thinking back to those days, said he did not recall that anyone told him the extent of his injuries or how they occurred. He felt weak, faint and a bit dazed. He was in the care of what appeared to be very competent medical caregivers, and he yielded to their instructions.

"I remember being loaded on a hospital bus that soon was en route to an airfield" and on the way to Tokyo, the powerless young wounded soldier recalled. He remembered one incident during that during the trip when a wounded Turkish soldier "was very vocal about saying that the Turks are 'Number One' and GI's are 'Number 10,' an expression he probably picked up in Japan." Sergeant Floyd suggested that phrase might have been the only English words the Turkish soldier knew.

During the admission procedures at a hospital in Tokyo, Joe Mac said that a noncommissioned officer asked, "Do you have any money?" He explained that any money would be locked in hospital ward safe for security. Joe Mac recalled saying, "250," and that the NCO started to give him a form to fill out. The amount was clarified when Sergeant Floyd said, "$2.50," to which the hospital NCO said, "xxxx, forget it," and moved on.

"That was all the money I had," Joe Mac recalled. He would not have additional money for several days.

"I didn't know what treatment I had received at the MASH unit or the 121st Evacuation Hospital," Sergeant Floyd remembered, adding, "The only thing I knew was that my left hand was in a cast. I didn't know they had shaved my head in order to remove bone from my forehead."

After being assigned to a ward, Sergeant Floyd said that he was allowed—or more accurately was expected—to get out of bed and move around the ward. The first time he went into the latrine, he was stunned. There was a mirror just inside the door and that was the first time that he was able to see just how he looked.

"I was thin from loss of weight, my head had been shaved and it looked like they had removed half of my head. Boy, what a shock!" he said.


Upon arrival at a military hospital in Tokyo, Japan, the injured soldier was scheduled for surgery and told that surgeons were going to "treat my hand."

Although prepared for surgery, given anesthesia, and "wheeled into the operating room," the scheduled surgery did not occur. Joe Mac recalled, "When I finally woke up, I was told that they did nothing because the hand was healing well."

That of course was not true. Upon closer examination, the surgeons had realized that major reconstruction of the hand was necessary. Joe Mac presumed that "the doctors at the Tokyo hospital either did not have the time—or the skill—to undertake such a surgery."

Joe Mac was unable to take care of some of his needs and remembered that while in the Tokyo hospital a volunteer WAC came by his bed and offered to give him a shave. He said that as he reclined in his hospital bed, the WAC used a safety razor to give him the first shave in several days.

"I really needed that and I really appreciated the shave," Joe Mac commented.


Evacuation back "to the States" was planned for the more seriously wounded who were being treated at the Tokyo hospital. Joe Mac and others were taken by hospital bus to the airport and loaded on a plane. The expected take off did not occur because of engine trouble, and the patients were unloaded and told they would spend the night in the airport dispensary.

"I hadn't noticed before, but when we got to the dispensary and were assigned beds, I realized that about half of the patients were mental cases, complete with leather cuffs on arms and legs," Joe Mac related. He added, "I didn't know their true condition, so I spent a rather sleepless night."

When the patients were placed on board the plane the next morning, Joe Mac said "only a few of the mental patients were on my flight."

The plane made a stop in Hawaii, where "lovely young Hawaiian ladies," each with a flower over one ear, met the wounded soldiers and welcomed each patient with a "lei."

Joe Mac said he missed out on a more entertaining visit from the young ladies of the islands who came to visit and perform for the patients at Tripper General Hospital. He recalled, with some disappointment, that when he got settled in the ward that he went to the latrine for a shower.

"While I was in the latrine, a group of young ladies came to the ward to entertain and performed their traditional hula dance," he related, and then added, "I was showering and missed all of it!"

During all these days, Joe Mac was traveling without much money—only the $2.50 in military script. He explained that he had missed the pay call at the end of December, but while in Hawaii was able to get partial pay of about $40.00.

"This added to the occupation script would be my traveling home money," Joe Mac advised.


From Hawaii, Joe Mac was flown to Travis Air Force Base in California, but was soon evacuated to Brooke Army Hospital at Fort Sam Houston in San Antonio,

Texas. This was to be his treatment center, and he was able to telephone his parents and let them know where he would be stationed for the next few weeks or months.

All patients coming from Korea were assigned a code name, "Project Raven." This was printed on the identification card attached to the foot of the hospital bed.

At Brooke Army Hospital, Joe Mac was assigned first to the neurology ward, where numerous diagnostic tests and examinations were performed to determine if he had brain damage. Those tests confirmed that he did not have brain damage. His skull had been shattered, but the brain was not damaged.

Joe Mac recalled "the doctors in the neurology ward talked to me more than anyone on the evacuation route."

It was here that he finally learned what had caused his injuries. He was told that a trip flare had detonated and fragments had struck his head and hand. This was his first knowledge of what happened that day in Korea. Joe Mac said that while in the hospital he met several other patients whose injuries also had been caused by trip flare explosions—many with injuries more severe than his.

The standard uniform for travel and the hospital time had been pajamas, a thin robe and a pair of cloth slippers. The patients were always transported on litters that were held in racks in the bus, plane or ambulance. There was little need for any other clothing than the hospital apparel.

In anticipation that some patients would in time be able to leave the hospital for brief periods, arrangements were made for uniforms to be issued. Joe Mac remembered that he was "sent across the post" to a supply center for an issue of new clothing.

"I walked to the supply center in my pajamas, robe and cloth slippers and walked back in the same dress, carrying a duffle bag containing my new uniforms," he said.

The clothing was checked into a storeroom, since patients were not permitted to wear uniforms in the hospital wards. Uniforms would be "checked out of storage" when or if a patient received a pass or short leave.

For Joe Mac, that would be a long time in the future.


Examinations were finally completed in the neurology department and Joe Mac was transferred to the orthopedic department in another building at Brooke Army Hospital. Orthopedic surgeons determined that the metacarpal bones of Joe Mac's left hand were broken and they proceeded to set the bones using a combination of bone grafts and wire.

Joe Mac said that the doctors always talked to him either before or after surgery to carefully explain what they planned to do or had done.

"I thought this was very considerate of the medical staff," Joe Mac remarked in reflecting on his hospital stay.

During the lengthy period of recuperation, Joe Mac and others in the hospital moved around the hospital wearing convalescent clothes—waist length jackets and trousers, blue or maroon colors, and with the Medical Corps insignia on the left side.

"We seldom, if ever, had a good fit," Joe Mac observed.

Joe Mac had always been a bit on the slender side, but during the weeks of illness and treatment, he had become very thin. With good food provided, and patients permitted to eat as much as they desired, Joe Mac began to regain some weight.

The surgery on his hand was successful, but after the cast was removed he could not move his fingers up or down. They remained in a slight cupped position.

The medical staff members were quick to say, "It is all in your head," Joe Mac recalled.

"Psychological or not," Joe Mac said, "I could not move my fingers."

The next stop, thus, was at the brace shop where the craftsman designed a device called a "knuckle buster" that was placed on the hand to apply tension through rubber bands that forced the fingers downward.

"I wore that device several hours a day," Joe Mac said. He added that with the brace, hydrotherapy and massage therapy, he began to regain the range of motion. The fingers, though, could be bent downward, but he could not raise them.

So, he was sent back to the brace shop for a device that was strapped to the top of his arm and had four extensions out over the fingers. Attached to the extensions were rubber bands with leather loops—one loop for each finger. This tension would pull the fingers upward.

Occupational therapy was scheduled and Joe Mac began working in leather craft and making silver jewelry. The use of his left hand increased in range of motion.

Using a promise of "a leave" as an incentive, the medical staff gave Joe Mac a challenge, "Make a fist and you can have a leave."

"I finally got a leave," Joe Mac recalled. He would get out of the hospital—even though briefly.


The medical staff advised Joe Mac that he should wait about six months or so after the first surgery on his head before a metal plate could be implanted. Sometime in May 1952, the surgery to implant the metal plate was scheduled.

The metal plate was made in the very busy hospital brace shop. The operation was successful. A small scar across the forehead—hardly noticeable—was the only outward indication of the serious head injury.

Joe Mac recalled, "When I got to the brace shop and sat down on a stool, the craftsman took a pen with water-soluble ink and drew a line around the area on my forehead where the bone had been removed."

The process was continued as the talented medical specialist took a piece of moistened chamois leather and pressed it to Joe Mac's forehead. The water-soluble ink transferred to the chamois and served as a pattern for the future plate.

Joe Mac, who later became a talented educator who taught students some metalwork skills, remembered that the technician used scissors to cut out the pattern that was then placed on piece of sheet metal. A simple awl was used to mark the shape and Joe Mac recalled watching the metal craftsman as he "cut the plate from the metal with tin snips."

"The craftsman placed the metal plate on a canvas bag filled with small steel balls (shot bag) and using the peen end of a ball-peen hammer tapped the metal to the correct shape," Joe Mac related.

Joe Mac remembered that the technician "would hold the plate up to my forehead from time to time to get the correct contours."

After the plate was tapped to the proper shape, several holes were drilled into the plate to prevent heat build-up.

Joe Mac said that when the craftsman seemed to be satisfied with the work, "he pitched the plate to me and told me to take it back to the ward and they would sterilize it in the autoclave."

And "That," Joe Mac summarized, "is the way my precision metal implant was fabricated,"

The hand crafted, custom-designed plate was effective.

During review by the Physical Evaluation Board, Joe Mac initially was awarded a 60% permanent service connected disability and given a Medical retirement at the age of 19. The retirement was effective August 31, 1952, exactly two years from his induction to active duty. Later, the Veterans Administration evaluated Joe Mac and increased the disability to 70%.

In addition to the metal plate to protect the brain area, Joe Mac lost two knuckles on his left hand and lost the feeling in his left index finger due to nerve damage. Through rehabilitation effort, he was able to compensate for that damage.

After returning to Oklahoma, Joe Mac Floyd began planning for his future.

He entered East Central State College (now East Central University) in Ada, Oklahoma, in August 1952. While at East Central, he met and married the former LaVerne Baldwin from Paoli, Oklahoma. After graduating with a Bachelor of Science degree and obtaining teaching credentials, the Floyds moved to Stillwater to attend the Graduate School of Oklahoma A&M College (now Oklahoma State University).

After completing a Master of Science degree in 1956, Joe Mac taught school at Ada Junior High School, the same school he, his brother and many friends had attended many years earlier.

Joe Mac and LaVerne began their family. When their two children were beginning elementary school, LaVerne returned to school and completed two degrees—a bachelor of science in medical technology and the second degree in education.

Joe Mac later decided to pursue additional graduate studies and in 1964 began studies in a doctoral program at Texas A&M University, College Station, Texas. He and his wife both taught in area public schools while Joe Mac studied for the advanced Ph.D. degree. One year later, Joe Mac began fulltime study at Texas A&M, became a graduate school teaching assistant, and then completed his doctorial degree in industrial education and technology.

The degrees and teaching experience opened the way for his appointment to the Industrial Technology Department of the College of Engineering at Tennessee Technology University, Cookeville, Tennessee, in 1966. He taught there until his retirement with Emeritus Professor status in 1995 after three decades at the university.

During a huge retirement ceremony and dinner that was attended by friends, faculty and students, Joe Mac was also honored with the establishment of the "Joe M. Floyd Endowment Fund" that provides scholarships for Industrial Technology students to attend Tennessee Technological University.

In the meantime, LaVerne Floyd enjoyed a career in higher education and then some key executive assignments with International Clinical Laboratories, Inc. (ICL) that opened a private school in Cookeville, Tennessee, to educate and train clinical laboratory technicians.

In 1980, after ten years of working for ICL, she bought the school, expanded operations, added campuses in Nashville, Tennessee, and Baton Rouge, Louisiana. The schools were successful and in 2000, the schools were sold, providing an opportunity for the Floyds to invest in commercial and residential rental properties, keeping both busy, even during retirement years.

Following his retirement from the University, Joe Mac and their son bought a 25-acre farm in Belize, Central America, with the intent of developing a 1,300-tree orange grove. A farmhouse was built on the property.

A hurricane wiped out that farming operation and the home and farm became a vacation spot for the family— sometimes used, but with promises to go there more often in the future.

Joe Mac, reflecting on the years since Korea, properly summarized those years with these words:

"All in all, we have had a good life!"

That might be an understatement for a man who many thought would never survive the injuries received on the side of a snow-covered mountain in North Korea more than five decades ago.

*Company C, 180h Infantry Regiment, moved into front line positions in early December 1951, after relieving units of the 1ˢᵗ Cavalry Division. Rifle platoons were deployed along steep hills and ridges overlooking the Yokkuk-ch'on River and scattered across former rice paddy farmland in the river valley. Outposts were placed on the strategic Arrowhead ridge, north side of the river. Sergeant Joe Mac Floyd was with his rifle squad on the forward (north) slope of the steep hill in the center of this map when he became Company C's first casualty of the war. Route of the rescue effort is indicated by ◄◄◄◄ symbols.*

*(Military Operations Map, 180ᵗʰ Infantry Regiment, Archives, 45ᵗʰ Infantry Division Museum)*

165

*The AP Rescue Photograph—*
*Human Chain To Save a Life.*

*An Associated Press photographer captured on film the valiant action of the soldiers linked hand-to-hand in the rescue effort in a news photograph taken of the rescuers struggling in the snow as they approached the top of the hill.*

*The climb to the top of the hill required mountain-climbing skills, using hands and feet to pull and push up the almost 60-degree slope. Doing so with a rifle strung across the shoulder or carrying other fighting equipment was difficult in itself.*

*Among those in the human chain of rescuers were Sergeant First Class Joe Dunham; Sergeant First Class Joe Hill Floyd, a cousin of the wounded soldier; Sergeant First Class Benny C. Floyd, the injured soldier's brother, all of Ada, Oklahoma; Private First Class Earl J. Lebouf, Theriot, Louisiana; Corporal Robert D. Fitzjerrell, North Little Rock, Arkansas; Private First Class Nolan N. Blount, Albany, Louisiana; Corporal Edward J. Bankos, Boonton, New Jersey; Private First Class Pablo Velasquez, Price, Utah; Private First Class Edgar L. Schmidt, Milwaukee, Wisconsin; and Corporal Kemper W. Chambers, Rockaway, New Jersey.*

*The valiant combat medic who provided the life-saving first medical assistance to Sergeant JoeMac Floyd was Private First Class Duane M. Laws, Mexico, New York.*

*(December 1951)*

*(Associated Press Wirephoto. Copyright, January 4, 1952)*

*The front edge of the three-pound steel helmet worn by Sergeant Joe Mac Floyd was blown upward and badly bent from the explosion that tore into his head. The helmet most likely saved his life. The now famous M1 "steel pot" design used during the Korean War was adopted in 1941 to replace the M1917 helmet that remained largely unchanged since the First World War. It was of two-piece design with an outer Hadfield steel shell and a separate inner liner containing the suspension system and a web chinstrap with a breakaway release.*

*(Photo courtesy of Joe Mac Floyd)*

*The Floyds—brothers and cousin—at Camp Chitose, Japan, in November 1951 just days before Company C departed for Korea. Brothers, Sergeant First Class Benny C. Floyd (left) and Sergeant Joe Mac Floyd (right), flank their cousin, Sergeant First Class Joe Hill Floyd.*

*(Photo courtesy of Joe Mac Floyd).*

*Sergeant Joe Mac Floyd, with steel plate in his head, wounds healing and new hair growing over head wounds, was on the road to recovery in early Summer 1952. He was given medical retirement from active duty on August 31, 1952, at age 19.*

*(Photo courtesy of Joe Mac Floyd)*

# Chapter Eleven

## Death of an Infantryman—

For whatever reason—whether because of my assignment as the unit administrative officer, my somewhat limited training and experience as a writer, my daily use of the unit's battered portable typewriter to maintain the unit's records, the daily reports and other writings, or because the company commander simply didn't feel comfortable with the task—the heart-tugging assignment of writing the parents of a soldier who died in action was mine.

Captain Garnet E. Mercer, who hailed from War, West Virginia, was a tough as nails Infantry officer and a decorated veteran of World War II where he served in Europe with the 38th Armored Infantry Battalion in the Seventh Armored Division. He was enjoying civilian life after the war when he suddenly was called back to active duty at the start of the Korean War. He was assigned as the new company commander of Company C, 180th Infantry Regiment, shortly after our unit arrived in Korea.

Having an experienced combat officer leading the unit was reassuring to those of us who were about to get our first taste of battle. Our long-time commander and home-town acquaintance, Captain Lawrence Craig McBroom, had been reassigned as commanding officer of Headquarters Company, First Battalion, temporarily turning command to First Lieutenant Howard Nicks, a newspaper editor from Wetumka, Oklahoma, who had served as executive officer and was a popular and respected officer, well suited for command responsibility.

When the higher-ranking Captain Mercer was assigned to the battalion, he became the new Company C commander, and Lieutenant Nicks, continued as executive officer for a bit longer, but soon was promoted to Captain and became company commander of another infantry company. Lieutenant Raymond Parnell, an ex-paratrooper turned to "straight-leg" infantry, was chosen to be the new "Exec."

Private First Class Ralph DiPalma was a draftee of Italian ancestry who had received his Presidential "Greetings" in his hometown of Newark, New Jersey, and, along with scores of other draftees, was shipped to then Camp Polk, Louisiana, to help bring the newly-activated 45th Infantry Division to combat strength, and to participate in a fast-track combat training to see how quickly such a division could be properly prepared for war.

DiPalma was two or three years older than some of the draftees, slightly overweight, and with bad eyesight that required his wearing thick-lens glasses that seemed to indicate his vision probably was not suitable for a person assigned to duty as a light weapons infantryman, the military occupation specialty given soldiers with duty in infantry rifle companies. He might have been better suited for duty in a non-combat service unit had the induction center staff been more careful in the assignment of new draftees.

Nevertheless, he was an infantryman in Company C, trained hard with the unit in Louisiana and in Japan, earned his first stripe as a private first class before the unit left Japan for Korea, and was serving faithfully when he was killed in action on a cold winter night in February 1952 while on a patrol on a ridge of T-Bone Hill in North Korea.

He was 10,000 miles from home.

Other members of the patrol carried his body back to the company's position.


My letter to Mr. and Mrs. DiPalma in Newark, New Jersey, to give them a bit more information about their son's death than was contained in the cold telegram they received earlier, was written and rewritten by me after careful thought and much prayer.

The letter spoke of how their son, Ralph, was well-liked by others in his infantry platoon, of his brave service, of his love for family and country, and expressed the sympathy of all of us in the unit. Most likely the letter was of little comfort to a bereaved family.

Ralph DiPalma was 25 years old at the time of his death. I wondered about whether the vision difficulty and those thick-lens glasses he had to wear might in some way have contributed to his death. He was wearing those glasses that night. I packed the glasses with other personal items from his pack and duffle bag in a small container for shipment back to his family.

All the belongings of a soldier while in a front line assignment are stuffed into a duffle bag and pack, some of the belongings temporarily stored in the unit's supply area. Sorting through and inventorying the belongings to separate personal items from military issue is a strange experience.

That, too, was my assignment. I asked another non-commissioned officer to be present and to assist in that process. Everything in the bag was considered. Pictures, notes, scraps of paper, shaving and personal grooming items, snacks, letters, billfold, rings, watch and seemingly scores of other items are accumulated and mixed among the uniforms, socks, underwear, sweater and other GI gear.

Each item was examined and considered. What to send home? What to return to the unit supply sergeant for reprocessing or possible reissue to another soldier? What to destroy?

I remember one unusual item that was found in Ralph DiPalma's belongings—a carefully wrapped stick of seasoned Italian salami, obviously shipped to him by his family back home in New Jersey. He had been saving that prized food item for a time when he could really savor the food that would remind him of home.

What to do?

I placed the food delicacy aside and then, after discussion with others the next morning, reasoned that Private First Class DiPalma would want to share that food gift from home with his friends on the front lines in Korea.

That was the decision. Thus, with stale C-ration crackers from the 1945-era combat rations that had been packaged for soldiers fighting a previous war, the special roll of meat was sliced and enjoyed by a half-dozen soldiers, sitting in a circle—eating salami and crackers, and remembering Ralph DiPalma.

Most of the rest of that group would live to be old men.

Ralph DiPalma would be 25 years old forever.

# Chapter Twelve

## Lonely Walk—

Being alone in the middle of the night on a snow-packed trail in the mountains of North Korea can be a bit unsettling. Landmarks that are familiar during daylight hours are not readily identified at night—especially a cloudy, moonless night.

The once deep snow of a few weeks earlier had begun to thin a bit with some warmer daytime temperatures and from the wind whipping down the valleys where the trails and narrow roads were located. The trail-like roads had once linked small Korean villages and tiny farms. The villages had been reduced to piles of rubble during the previous year. Many of the names along the trails—Taeho-dong, Sonbyok, Unhoeng, Yutchon-ni and Chura-dong—remained on the Army maps. The people who once lived in those villages, at least those who had survived, had fled the area long ago.

This ground on which I walked was an area where just a few months earlier, in late fall, the famed 1st Cavalry Division had battled Chinese and North Korean armies. An irregular line had been drawn across the military maps. On the ground, that line became the Main Line of Resistance) (MLR) now occupied by my company and other units of the 45th Infantry Division.

Although my concerns may not have been fully justified, some major fears gnawed at me that night.

During the weeks before this night, as armies fought a series of seesaw battles to take and hold the high ground and establish defensive positions, land mines had been placed in the ground along trails and in other areas. A few weeks later, the ground became frozen and later covered by ice and snow.

Most likely, some of those mines remained hidden beneath the snow and frozen surface.

Since early November, when sub-freezing weather arrived and the snow began to cover the ground, the roads and trails often were challenging for drivers—and passengers.

Now as the wind whipped into the valleys and the snow began disappearing in places, a nagging question came to my mind: "Would the tiny prongs that trigger anti-personnel land mines now be exposed?"

Each step that I look was with the thought in mind that a small anti-personnel mine might be triggered and I would be killed instantly or disabled—a foot or leg blown to smithereens.

I had traveled along this narrow road during daylight hours. This was the first time I had been on foot in the area. Now, it was nighttime, I was alone, not quite sure of my exact location, and gingerly walking back to my unit that was deployed in defensive positions along the MLR.

There was one connecting trail that I must locate in order to reach my unit. The need to find the second trail gave cause to the second fear I held that night.

Elements of the First Battalion, 180th Infantry Regiment, were deployed in defensive positions along the ridges of small mountains, having moved into the positions after a three or four week assignment in reserve where the unit had spent some time in rest, equipment maintenance, and continued training in preparation for a new assignment.

Now, the unit was back in front line positions.

The men of Company C occupied bunkers, outposts, foxholes and some trench positions. Part of the unit was deployed along a narrow finger of a ridge that led off into a larger river valley. The finger of land pointed toward a small hill in the valley that often "changed hands" as American forces and Chinese forces alternately probed defensive positions and took position of the hill.

That hill began to be called "T-bone Hill" because on a map the terrain contour lines very much resembled the shape of a nice T-bone steak. A few weeks later, in March 1952, a fierce battle between Chinese forces and another unit of the 180h Infantry Regiment erupted over possession of "Outpost Eerie" located on a ridge of that hill.

Many brave men were killed or wounded in that fight.

That battle, though, was a few weeks in the future from the night I walked alone along the trail.

The trail along which I now walked was once a road between small villages that were in the area.

As I walked, I recalled that the connecting trail I needed to locate was one that intersected on the right side, almost at a 90-degree angle, and led to Company C's assigned sector.

Near that intersection of trails, a half-track vehicle of the 145th AAA battalion, an anti-aircraft unit, had been deployed. The quad 50-caliber machineguns were aimed skyward to fire at enemy airplanes that might, but most likely would not, sweep from the sky to bomb or strafe our nearby positions.

During daylight hours, I had been able to see the AAA half-track tucked away in its slightly camouflaged location.

Several questions came to mind:

"Would I be able to see the half-track vehicle now in the pitch-dark hours of near midnight?" and, "Would the soldiers who were assigned to that anti-aircraft unit be alerted by me—a solitary soldier who, as far as they knew, could be a Chinese infiltrator seeking to get behind the lines?"

I also wondered about these other issues:

"Would the soldiers shoot first, or would they call out for a password?"

"Did I know the right password for the day?"

"Did the password change a midnight or daylight the next morning?"

I wasn't sure about the password.

Getting by that position was not my greatest fear at that moment. This thought came to mind: "What if I were to miss that intersection of trails and remain on the road, moving on West? North? Northwest?"

The narrow road led through a gap between two small mountains and into "No Man's Land" between our line of defense and the line of defense of the Chinese units.

Just a short distance from that point was another unusually shaped hill that also, a few months later, would be another major battle site—Pork Chop Hill. At the moment, Chinese forces held that ridge.

During the period from December 1951 to June 1952, the Division's 179th and 180th Infantry Regiments fought repeatedly over Pork Chop Hill. Even after the 45th Division was relocated to the Eastern side of the Korean peninsula, possession of this key piece of terrain that seemed to control the area was still hotly contested.

That was a dangerous area and I didn't want to wander into the shadows of Pork Chop Hill in the middle of the night, all alone.

If I missed the intersection of trails, I would end up in an area where I most likely would be killed or captured.


How did I get into this predicament?

Earlier in the day in order to handle some administrative matters for the unit, I made my way to the regimental headquarters a few miles south of our front line positions in an open Jeep, the well-known and beloved Army utility vehicle.

With me was Private First Class Charles E. Allen, our unit headquarters section driver. Private Allen, a cheerful Southerner who hailed from Choudrant, Louisiana, was a lumberjack-logger in the pine forests of northern Louisiana before he was drafted into the Army just a few weeks after the start of the Korean War. He was among the first group of draftees to arrive at Camp Polk, Louisiana, in November 1950 and then assigned to Company C.

His hometown was really a small village of about 500 people located in Lincoln Parish, not far from the larger city of Ruston, in northern Louisiana.

Some would describe Private Allen as a "giant of a man." He was tall and strong, but a gentle bear of a man with a great sense of humor. He also was one of the finest Army drivers around, even if he had experienced a bit of difficulty on one or two occasions remembering to "drive on the left side" of the roads during our months in Japan before our unit left for Korea.

"People just don't drive on that side of the road in Louisiana," he would remind me on each of our close calls on some of the rural roads in the area outside of Chitose on Japan's northernmost island of Hokkaido where our unit served prior to departing to Korea.

179

Private Charles Allen and I had covered many miles together during the months of service in Japan and now in Korea as he faithfully performed his duties as the administrative section driver at the wheel of the rugged little Jeep, the famous quarter-ton general purpose, four-wheel drive vehicle first used during World War II, and now the workhorse utility vehicle for those of us in Korea.

It was it in that role that Private Allen responded to my call late in the afternoon that winter day when company commander Captain Garnet E. Mercer dispatched me to the 180th Infantry Regiment's forward headquarters location with some messages and documents that needed prompt delivery.

The regimental headquarters was located a few miles southeast of the front line location. The trip would extend into nighttime hours.

During the late night return trip, somewhere in the vicinity of the rubble of what was once the village of Ch'abo-chip, the Jeep's engine sputtered and "died." Nothing worked. Every effort to restart the engine failed—even our slip and slide attempt to "push-start" the Jeep on the snow-covered road.

Although the drivers and mechanics worked diligently to keep all the unit's vehicles ready for service, they had some challenges—thanks to the Army's decision concerning transfer of equipment between units that were in Korea.

When the first units of the 45th Division packed to depart Japan for Korea, the orders were to leave all our top-quality vehicles, large weapons and heavy equipment in Japan and to accept ownership of the vehicles, weapons and heavy equipment in use by the units of the 1st Cavalry Division in Korea—the units that were being relieved "in place" along the front lines in Korea and sent to Japan.

These two Army divisions were trading places and missions, as well as vehicles and equipment. The idea

180

seemed reasonable. There was a major problem though—the vehicles, weapons and heavy equipment that were being inherited from the 1st Cavalry Division were "war-weary."

The Thunderbird division had pristine vehicles and equipment in Hokkaido. The vehicles received in the exchange in Korea were hardly in that category.

In the months just prior to this exchange of troops and equipment, units of the 1st Cavalry Division had been in several hard-fought battles in North Korea. The "Jamestown Line" that now marked the main line of resistance (MLR) was established in October 1951, just two months before our unit arrived to begin the replacement of the 1st Cavalry Division troops.

The vehicles and equipment turned over to the 45th Division showed the wear and tear of severe service. Many vehicles and heavy weapons needed major overhaul work or replacement.

The Jeep in which Private Allen and I were traveling that night was just a "weary" vehicle that had reached a breaking point. No one could be blamed. The Jeep had become another "casualty" of the war.

What to do? Three or four options were considered. We could leave the vehicle unattended and walk to the unit. One of us could stay with the vehicle and the other walk to the unit. We could wait until daylight when other military traffic would come along the road and stop to assist.

After brief discussion, I suggested that Allen remain with the Jeep while I walked to the unit and sent others to help repair or retrieve the Jeep and Private Allen.

Thus began the lonely walk.


Despite my fear of being lost and possibly captured, or of being killed or maimed by a land mine, or being shot by friendly troops because I did not remember a password, none of those things happened.

The connecting trail was located. The gunners who manned the AAA halftrack that guarded that part of the valley—and the sky above—did not challenge my passage. I walked the final half-mile or so to Company C's headquarters area and began disturbing others to help bring Private Allen—and the ailing Jeep—back home.

That mission was accomplished a few hours later. Life in a rifle company in Korea returned to normal.

Fear is real. And, fear in a war zone is perhaps more understandable, even if immediate conditions may not demand or support that feeling.

A person can become immobilized by fear if it is permitted to take charge of mind and behavior. But, if a person has never had fear, he may have difficulty learning courage—that ability to face danger, difficulty and uncertainty.

Fear and courage go together hand in hand.

I learned a little bit more about both—fear and courage—on the lonely walk.

*A halftrack from the145ᵗʰ Anti-Aircraft Artillery (AAA) Battalion provided front line air defense with its Quad 50-caliber machine-guns. The halftrack's position was a critical point on the "lonely walk."*         *(March 1952)*

*Company headquarters section driver Private First Class Charles E. Allen of Choudrant, Louisiana, and Oliver covered many miles together in a Jeep.*

*This narrow snow-covered trail leading to Company C's front line position became difficult to find and follow on a cloudy, moonless winter night.*

*(February 1952)*

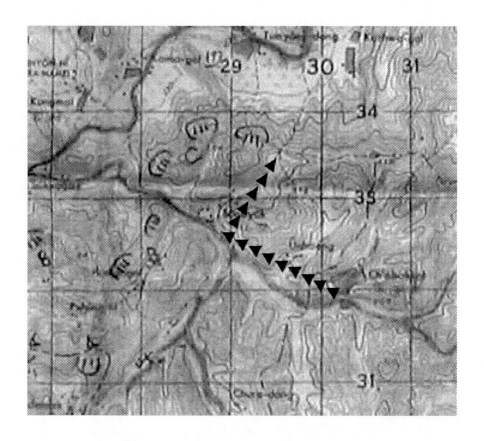

*Company C, 180ᵗʰ Infantry Regiment, occupied front line positions in an area east of Pork Chop Hill and slightly south of T-bone Hill in February 1952, as indicated on the area map. The route of the lonely walk was along the trail near the rubble of what had once been Ch'abo-chip village. The walk route is indicated by ◀◀◀◀ symbols.*

*(Military Operations Map, 180ᵗʰ Infantry Regiment, Archives, 45ᵗʰ Infantry Division Museum)*

# Chapter Thirteen

## Tony Dufflebag—

As we moved through the small villages scattered in the area north of Seoul on the way to the front, the extreme difficulties faced by the Korean civilians whose land was being ravaged by war became very clear. These people were struggling to survive.

The plight of the small children tugged at our hearts. They were suffering most of all.

Many of us riding in those trucks and Jeeps were fathers with small children back home. Seeing the poorly clad, cold and hungry children standing outside the huts or in the streets of villages reminded all of us soldiers of our own children back home

There was a big difference, though. Our children in the United States were safe, secure, well fed, warm and properly clothed. Just the opposite was the plight for the Korean children.

Our silent question was: "What would happen to these Korean children?"

As our convoy of military vehicles rolled by, the observing people stared. The faces of the Korean children, for the most part, were blank of expression except for what could be detected in those dark, penetrating eyes. The eyes were wide open and observing everything.

I could not forget the eyes.

Our convoy of trucks moved closer to front line positions, far beyond the area where civilians were living. Darkness fell, and for the moment, any thoughts of children in distress were quickly replaced with the more immediate concerns of impending combat and the enemy troops occupying those mountains and hills now looming before us.

At the time, none of us knew that some unusual circumstances soon would bring us into close personal contact with one of those Korean children who would steal the hearts of the men of Company C.

During late February or early March 1952, four soldiers from Company C were authorized a short rest and recuperation leave that would permit them to spend two or three days in Seoul, the heavily-damaged capital city of South Korea. The four soldiers chosen for the short leave were Sergeant First Class Joe Hill Floyd, Sergeant First Class James A. West, Sergeant Bob G. Jones and Sgt John C. Matthews.

Sergeants Floyd and West were being recognized for recent heroic combat action for which both were being recommended for the Bronze Star Medal for valor. Sergeant Jones, believed by Company C troops to be one of the finest "mess sergeants" in the United States Army, was noted for being able to produce great meals, including bakery items, from a field kitchen even under the most severe conditions. And Sergeant Matthews, a World War II veteran and recently awarded his second Combat Infantryman's Badge, was being honored for his unusual supply sergeant skills in finding equipment and supplies for the company, through official and unofficial means.

Even though the Korean capital city of Seoul was still a bombed out city, the four men were anxious to get away from the front lines with the prospects of a short stay in a hotel, with real beds, real showers, a restaurant, and to see the sights of a large city that was beginning to return to life.

Their hotel proved to be an unusual one—the German Embassy. The beds, showers and meals, though, were provided and enjoyed. Their lives—and the lives of many others in Company C—would be impacted in a most unusual way as the result of that trip.

When the four soldiers returned to the unit three days later, they brought with them a most unusual "package," tucked away inside a duffle bag.

Friends gathered when the four men returned to the unit. Everyone was eager to hear of their experiences during their brief visit to Seoul.

Sergeant Floyd unsnapped the top of his duffle bag and pulled forth a tiny, grinning Korean boy who appeared to be about six or seven years old. They called him, "Tony." He understood that name, but few other English words. Questions and comments gushed forth almost at once from everyone gathered in a circle around the returning soldiers and Tony.

Chief among the questions were: "How did you get him by the Military Police checkpoints between Seoul and the front lines?" and "What are we going to do with him?"

Sergeants Floyd and West quickly began to answer the questions.

Sergeant Floyd remembered the story this way:

The brief rest and recuperation leave provided only two days in Seoul. The four men from Company C joined others from the regiment for a truck ride to a railhead, and then the group boarded a train for the trip to Seoul. They were assigned rooms in the German Embassy building, where Sergeants Floyd and West shared a large room with individual beds.

188

Sergeant Floyd recalled the first evening in Seoul and the rescue of Tony with these words:

"After checking into our room, we went out on the streets of Seoul to see the sights. As you can imagine, every building was shot up. There were a lot of people walking around and they were in a race to survive.

"Seoul, being on the northwestern border of South Korea, was the destination of all of the North Korean civilians who were escaping to the south. They were there with no aid or help of any kind. The South Korean government could not help its own refugees. One can imagine the turmoil that we saw as everyone scrambled to get food and shelter."

Sergeant Floyd related that the streets of Seoul were filled with children of various ages who were running around "begging for help." He said that most of these children were "lost, separated from their parents," and the children did not know if the parents were alive or dead.

During the early evening, Sergeants Floyd and West walked around the heavily-damaged business area of downtown Seoul looking at the people, the buildings and the sad conditions of the people and the city when they came upon a sight that that Sergeant Floyd said he would "never forget."

He described the moment with these words:

"Here was a young boy who was about six years old. He had freeze burn scabs on his body, the only clothes that he had on was two discarded undershirts, similar to what we would call muscle shirts today. One was wrapped around his waist and the other was over his shoulders. There was nothing on his feet.

"This kid was literally begging for his life. The temperature was in the teens. Sergeant West and I looked at each other and knew what we were going to do."

The two soldiers took the small Korean boy into a nearby shop where they bought him clothes, and then took him to a Korean bathhouse to see if they could get the child bathed.

Sergeant Floyd described the bathhouse as "a kind of swimming pool." They paid a Korean attendant to bathe the boy and the two soldiers then dressed him in the clothing they had purchased. Much of the clothing was too large, but rolled-up pants legs and shirtsleeves didn't matter. The boy was now clean, warm, and dressed.

Although the boy could not speak English, Sergeant Floyd said that "his eyes said it all" in expressing his feeling of gratitude that he could not put into words.

The next concern for the soldiers was getting some food into the stomach of a child who obviously had not eaten for a long time—perhaps even several days.

Sergeant Floyd continued the story in this manner:

"We then decided to feed him. On the way to a Korean restaurant, he saw a pile cap like Sergeant West and I were wearing, and we could tell that he wanted one. So we bought him one. We took him to a nice looking Korean restaurant. He didn't know how to order so we asked the waiter to bring him food. I have no idea how long it had been since he ate last but he ate everything they brought plus some refills."[13]

The major question of the evening, "Now what?" began to occupy the minds of both Sergeants Floyd and West. They had bathed the boy, clothed him, fed him, but didn't know anything about the boy, if he had a family, if he had a place to live. And, their knowledge of the Korean language was extremely limited.

They needed someone who could be a translator so they could ask the boy some questions about his parents or other relatives and then determine what do to next. The two soldiers, with the young boy between them, returned to the

---

[13] Floyd, Joe Hill. Personal correspondence to the author, December 9, 2004.

German Embassy where they found someone who could translate for them. The two soldiers wanted to help reunite the "little lost boy" with his parents or other relatives.

That was not to happen.

Sergeant Floyd said that through the translated conversation, the following story unfolded:

"Tony's parents had been killed by Chinese soldiers. He had no other relatives that he knew of. His Korean name sounded a bit like 'Tony.' Thus, that is where he got his first name."

Sergeants Floyd and West began inquiring about refugee housing in the area, but soon learned that none was available. The few places that did exist were filled to capacity and no one offered to take in another orphan boy off the streets. The streets were filled with such children.

Aware that if the young boy was simply left on the streets where they had found him that he would be robbed of his clothes in minutes by older children or by adults, Sergeant Floyd explained that he and Sergeant West decided to inquire if the boy could be housed with them that night in the Embassy.

When they talked with the Military Police guard who was on duty at the embassy gate about bringing Tony to stay the night, the guard advised them that his duties included inspecting duffle bags and other packages that are brought into the building to see if any "contraband" is contained in the bags. He also advised that as a practice, "every third bag" was inspected. The guard suggested that perhaps Sergeants Floyd and West "could help count bags" and perhaps miss an inspection of the duffle bag that one of them carried.

A solution was at hand.

On the street in front of the German Embassy on a cold night in March 1952, a young boy, who had just been given the name of "Tony," was stuffed inside a massive

Army duffle bag that was then carried into the lobby and up to the room assigned to Sergeants Floyd and West.

Sergeant Floyd asked fellow soldiers later, "Guess how 'Dufflebag' was acquired for a last name?"

Once inside the Embassy, arrangements were made for a cot and bedding to be brought to the room for Tony, and the lucky orphan boy off the streets of Seoul had his first sleep in a safe and warm place in a long time.

The following morning, the four soldiers from Company C joined those from other units and loaded onto trucks for a short trip to the railroad station, followed by a reverse journey by railroad and another truck ride back to the unit's positions in the mountains far north of Seoul.

Faced with the continuing need to conceal Tony from Military Police and other authorities, the young orphan boy was returned to the duffle bag hiding place as the soldiers boarded the truck, the train, and another truck for the final lap of the return journey. Fortunately, because of his tiny size, Tony had ample room to move amidst the few clothes and other items that Sergeant Floyd had carried with him for the short leave in Seoul.


Tony's life with Company C was good for him—and for all of us who had any part in his survival story.

After learning of the boy's presence, and listening to the circumstances of his rescue from the streets of Seoul, the company commander, Captain Garnet E. Mercer, demonstrated his fatherly traits and agreed to let Tony remain with the unit until battle conditions might change the circumstances. The commander authorized the issue of an additional cot for Sergeant Floyd's squad, and Tony had a new home—even though a temporary one.

Finding clothes small enough for a small Korean boy was a challenge. I wrote to my wife, Vinita, and asked her to buy some clothes and send them to us for Tony. Among items she sent was a Levi jean jacket. When it arrived, I sewed a "Thunderbird" division patch on the left sleeve, along with private first class strips on both sleeves. Tony was delighted with the Levi jacket and its perfect fit.

Wearing oversize fatigue pants, with pant legs rolled up several inches to keep from dragging the ground, with the Korean style cloth and leather shoes that Sergeants Floyd and West bought him in Seoul, with the dark-blue Levi jean jacket and topped off with an Army fatigue cap, bill flipped up in front and sitting cocked on his head, Tony was a picture of a happy kid.

Those seemed to be happy days for Tony. He didn't seem to have a care in the world.

None of us could really know, though. The language barrier was ever present.

During the days following Tony's arrival with the unit, soldiers throughout the company wrote home to tell their wives and parents of "the little orphan boy" who was with the company. Clothes, food and a few other items began to arrive in the mail for Tony. Someone sent him a "Hopalong Cassidy" two-gun holster set, complete with a belt with a big buckle.

Tony obviously felt the love of all the men in the company and demonstrated his appreciation of the care given to him by flashing an ever-present smile. He began to pick up bits and pieces of the English language, and soon was able to communicate some of his thoughts.

His very special friends, though, were Sergeants Floyd and West, the two men who had rescued him in Seoul. During the time the unit remained in front line positions, Tony's temporary home was in the company headquarters area. When conditions permitted, Tony could be observed climbing the hill to find Sergeants Floyd and West. When the company was relocated to a regimental reserve position in a much safer area, the company soldiers were permitted to sleep in large squad tents, and Tony moved his cot and small collection of belongings to the squad tent with Sergeants Floyd and West.

As word spread that a Korean child was with Company C, battalion and regimental officers often would arrive at the company headquarters with a mission to retrieve the child who obviously should not be in the custody of an Infantry unit in a combat zone.

During those visits, though, Tony simply "disappeared." The informal communications network among soldiers is unique. Someone in battalion headquarters always warned our unit that "the brass is on the way," and Tony would be taken to some hiding place.

This worked fine for several weeks until an order was issued by the battalion commander advising Company C's commanding officer that Tony must be released to appropriate authorities so he could be placed in an orphanage. Captain Mercer was given a designated time and place to deliver the child to headquarters.

Sergeant Floyd recalled that his last time with Tony was during a chapel service that he attended with some of the men from Company C. The last bit of snow left from winter was melting and spring was returning to the battle-scarred Korean landscape. Sergeant Floyd wrote, "The last and best memory I have of Tony was sitting on the ground in a chapel service. Tony was pointing out some small yellow flowers" that were popping up through the melting snow.

Captain Mercer was a good officer, and obediently honored the orders.

Tony was gone.


In writing about the Korean War, one newspaper reporter expressed the thoughts that "in a country devastated by war, it is usually the children who suffer most. Thunderbird men realized this and made unfortunate Korean orphans their special charge."[14]

The soldiers of Company C continued to think about Tony during the days that followed, but there also was a war to fight. None of us heard just what happened to Tony after he was handed over to battalion leaders.

All of us knew that keeping Tony with the unit in a combat zone was neither safe nor appropriate. Tony needed to be in a place where he could be safe, with other children, and where he could begin receiving an education.

Hopefully Tony was among those fortunate orphans who eventually were placed in a safe haven—perhaps on Cheyu-do, an island southeast of the Korean mainland. An orphanage was established there in what was once the Agriculture High School.

The orphanage, known as the "Orphans' Home of Korea," was founded in Seoul in 1950 by Madame On Soon Whang. Not long after it was formed, United States Air Force pilots and planes moved the group to Cheju-do.

That was a safer location.

After the war, the 45th Infantry Division leaders established a trust fund, administered by the 45th Infantry Division Association, to help provide financial support for the orphanage. A bronze plaque was placed at the orphanage, commemorating the aid given it by the "Thunderbirds."

In a letter to people in the United States after he became commanding general of the 45th Infantry Division, Major General P. D. Ginder wrote about the war's impact on the civilian population, explaining that they were "suffering almost as much as during actual fighting." He added, "Included in the civilian population are large numbers of children who for one reason or another have become orphans."

---

[14] Newspaper article (undated). Achieves, 45th Infantry Division Museum, Oklahoma City, Oklahoma.

"These children are one of the most tragic evidences of the cruel war which has been fought in their country."

"The Thunderbird Division has ...completed a collection taken from all units for the purpose of aiding certain established orphanages."

"Our campaign was most successful in that we raised over $50,000 for this worthy cause."... "to use in provide housing and supplementary food and medical assistance."

He asked for civilians in the United States to send clothing.

"The clothing campaign together with our (45ᵗʰ Division) efforts in providing facilities and food will further provide to the Korean people that the intent of the American people is that of kindness and helpfulness, demonstrating again the high ideals of our Democracy as opposed to the brutality of Communism which they have already witnessed."[15]


What became of Tony Dufflebag?

Did he grow to adulthood and become a leading citizen in his country as South Korea recovered from the devastation caused during the war?

During the years since those days in Korea I have wondered about Tony and have imagined various scenarios about what his life might have been like as he became a teenager, young adult and then into adulthood years.

Finding an adult "Tony" among the millions of people in South Korea seemed virtually impossible, especially when attempting to do so from halfway around the world.

During the mid 1970s as the result of our graduate school studies at the University of Tulsa, I became friends

---

[15] Memorandum (1953). Major General P.D. Ginder, Commanding General, 45ᵗʰ Infantry Division. Archives, 45ᵗʰ Infantry Division Museum, Oklahoma City, Oklahoma.

with a prominent Korean educator, Dr. Lee Dong Wook, who at the at time was a school administrator in Inch'on and later in Seoul, the South Korean capital city. The two of us received our Doctor of Educational Administration degrees together at the University of Tulsa.

The story of "Tony" was shared with Dr. Lee, along with my interest in attempting to locate the once small child who by then was an adult. My Korean friend advised me of the great difficulties involved in such a search. An inquiry to a newspaper editor in Seoul about publishing a story and picture in such a search effort went unanswered.

My educator friend, Dr. Lee, even invited me to visit with him and his family in Seoul in the summer of 1988 when the Olympic games were hosted by South Korea. My expenses would be limited simply to transportation and incidental costs, Dr. Lee informed me. His office was located only a few blocks from the Olympic stadium. He had connections and tickets. Dr. Lee promised free lodging and meals with his family. In addition to attending some of the Olympic competition, I could have made a personal effort to persuade a newspaper editor to assist with the search for Tony.

I was greatly tempted to make the trip. A variety of conditions related to work, health and family made such a trip extremely difficult and the kind offer of Dr. Lee and his family had to be declined.

Unfortunately, that became a missed opportunity.

Later, after his retirement and the death of his wife, Dr. Lee moved to San Francisco, California, to live with a child who had immigrated to the United States. He was in poor health.

The relocation resulted in both of us losing addresses and contact data, and the exchange of infrequent letters and holiday greeting cards ceased.

I learned later that he died soon after that relocation.

The search for an adult Tony was attempted again. During regular visits to speak at Oliver Middle School in Broken Arrow, Oklahoma, especially for special for Veterans Day assemblies or other patriotic events, I often was asked to speak to student groups about the Korean War and some of the experiences in that land. The rescue of Tony Dufflebag, with photographs of Tony and some of the soldiers of Company C, was among the stories frequently told—and always remembered by the young students.

One of the students who heard that story during her middle school years was Clara Suh, a young Korean girl whose family had immigrated to Broken Arrow. After she graduated from high school in 2005, Clara decided to seek her college education in her native homeland and returned to Seoul to attend a university.

She remembered the "Tony Dufflebag" story. After her arrival in Seoul, and with the assistance of one of Clara's favorite teachers at the middle school, Clara and I exchanged several email messages in which the two of us discussed how she might assist in persuading a newspaper editor in Seoul to print photographs and background information in an effort to find the adult Tony.

That effort has not been successful.


In a "feel good" movie screenplay or storybook ending of the tale, Tony would have become a great leader in South Korea, perhaps a national hero, a corporate giant or an elected officer of the land. At some point in such a story, he would have been reunited with some of the soldiers who rescued and befriended him as a child. Perhaps he would have visited the United States to meet the families of the soldiers who "adopted" him in Korea during those frightening days of his childhood.

The mind can imagine many dramatic stories.

198

Most likely, Tony really did become a person of significance in that nation. Even as a young child, Tony had an outgoing personality and a captivating smile, two essential elements for success in any profession.

An ancient Old Testament writer, Solomon, a Hebrew king, son and successor to King David, once wrote,

> *"A man's steps are directed by the Lord.*
> *How then can anyone understand his*
> *own way?"[16]*

Tony was rescued for a reason. He was destined for a good and purposeful life.

Perhaps someday all of us will know the rest of this story.


Tony Dufflebag owed his life to Joe Hill Floyd and James A. West. They rescued him from the streets of Seoul, Korea, when he was starving and freezing, and made a commitment to take him to a place of safety—with the soldiers of Company C.

James A. West, who was living in Oklahoma City, Oklahoma, died in late 2006. Joe Hill Floyd, living in Hobbs, New Mexico, died a few weeks later in January 2007.

Both were good soldiers—brave and true—and were good men.

They truly left the woodpile much higher than they found it!

---

[16] Proverbs 20:24

*Sergeant First Class Joe Hill Floyd, left, and Sergeant First Class James A. West, while on Rest and Recuperation leave in Seoul, South Korea, in early March 1952 rescued a starving young Korean boy from the streets of Seoul. Thus began the story of "Tony Duffle-bag."*

*(Photos courtesy of Joe Hill Floyd)*

*Tony Dufflebag shows a big smile while sitting on top a roll of barbed wire soon to be used in preparing defensive positions for Company C's front line positions.*

*(March 1952)*

*Tony Dufflebag and Master Sergeant Clarence G. Oliver, Jr., share time together in front of Company C's Command Post tent.*

*(March 1952)*

Tony felt he was a "real soldier" with M1 rifle and wearing a CIB.

(Photos courtesy of Harold Gene Evans)

First Sergeant Harold Gene Evans and Tony Dufflebag while in Regimental Reserve location.

(April 1952)

*Corporal Charles W. Crump of Ruston, Louisiana, a member of*
*Company C's second platoon, welcomes Tony Dufflebag during one of*
*Tony's visits to the second platoon's positions.*
*(Spring 1952)*
*(Photo courtesy Kemper W. Chambers)*

*Tony Dufflebag's time with Company C was about to end in April 1952. Soon after this photo was taken, Tony was picked up by staff officers from the 45th Infantry Division and sent to safety at an orphanage out of the combat zone. Tony is pictured "checking out" the weapons platoon's 57mm Recoilless Rifles.*

*(April 1952)*
*(Photo courtesy Kemper W. Chambers)*

# Chapter Fourteen

## God Knows—

Worship is a condition of the heart and mind. There isn't a requirement that one be in a church building.

During the years before and after the days in Korea, I worshipped in many churches—some small frame buildings, some beautiful church structures, once in a small log-walled chapel in the mountains of Montana, and, on a few special occasions, even joined in worship services in magnificent cathedrals.

No time of worship, though, has been more meaningful than the shared experience of a group of soldiers who huddled in a safe area on the reverse slope of a hill along the front lines in a combat zone, sitting on the ground, with helmets and rifles placed just inches away, and led by a beloved chaplain who offered words of encouragement and a voiced prayer asking God to place a protective hedge around us

Captain Ralph A. Purdy, chaplain for the 180th Infantry Regiment, was a fatherly Baptist preacher who would have looked more at home in a pulpit of a small community church than in combat gear in Korea. An Army Reserve officer, whose hometown was New Orleans, Louisiana, Chaplain Purdy was an ordained minister of the Northern (American) Baptist denomination.

The Korean War caught both the Army and the Chaplain's Corps off guard. There were only about 775 chaplains on active duty in the Army in 1950. With the start of the Korean War, there was a need to increase the number to 950 to meet the need of providing chaplains for the expanded size of the Army.

The Office of the Chief of Chaplains initiated an involuntary recall that included not only those chaplains who were activated with their Reserve and National Guard units, but also 240 chaplain Reservists who were individually ordered to active duty.

Within a year, the number of chaplains was increased to 1208. [17]

Captain Purdy was one of them.

Just how Ralph Purdy, who hailed from the heart of Southern Baptist country, came to be a minister of the Northern Baptist faith, was never shared with us. But, this man was our chaplain—the pastor of a strange and mixed flock of soldiers who were of many denominations and some who were of no denomination.

His enthusiastic prayers were lifted up to God, asking that a covering of safety be over all of us—many who might find themselves in a battle within a few hours.

During many of the weekly chapel services, my good friend and company clerk, Corporal Donald Peterson, used his professional talent as a trained musician to lead in the song services. In many Army units, the chaplain often doubled as both preacher and song leader. Chaplain Purdy, who had a loud but not quite so trained voice, was happy to en-

---

[17]Hourihan. < http://www.usachcs /brief/chapter_7.htm>

list the assistance of Corporal Peterson whose beautiful tenor voice greatly enhanced the services.

While our unit was in training in Japan, Chaplain Purdy led in weekly chapel services both in the field during maneuvers and at the sprawling tent city that bore the official name Camp Chitose where he ministered to and counseled soldiers throughout the regiment. During those months, he helped lead an effort to raise funds to build a church to be donated to the small, but growing, number of Japanese Christians living in the nearby city of Chitose.

I don't remember the exact amount of money that was raised for the church construction project, but believe that the total was in the range of $10,000.00, a significant sum in 1951. That church was built through the small contributions given by soldiers who attended the weekly chapel services during a period of several months prior to the 45th Division's deployment to Korea.

One doesn't have to be a "called missionary" to a foreign land to demonstrate some form of practical mission activity. The soldiers who contributed money and offered other support for this small congregation of Japanese Christians felt some need to take action to demonstrate in some manner our religious beliefs—to "walk the talk" of being a Christian, even though serving as soldiers in an Army of Occupation in a land of people who once were mortal enemies.

A target date of November 15, 1951, was set for completion of the new building. The volcanic ash block walls rose from the ground and the building was finished by the time the 45th Infantry Division left for Korea.

Mission accomplished!

The fledgling congregation of Christians in that small Japanese city was first organized under the leadership of Hiroshi Ito, the owner of a laundry in Chitose. The small group of Christians who lived in Chitose had started the building drive, but had limited success until the "Thunderbirds" joined in the effort.

After the success of the building drive was assured by the support of the soldiers, the Japanese church members were able to locate and employ a pastor who planned to move to Chitose from the nearby city of Otaru.

The church was built in the center of Chitose, near and overlooking the Chitose River, a beautiful stream that had been enjoyed by many of us during our off-duty visits into the nearby town.

Other people touch our lives, often in little ways that have life-long impact. Some of those experiences are remembered for the remainder of our lives.

Let me share one such experience.

In the days after Thanksgiving 1951, the men of Company C and all other units of the 180th Infantry Regiment, the lead elements of the 45th Infantry Division, climbed, aboard troop transport ships at the port city of Otaru on the island of Hokkaido, and headed toward Korea. The unit landed at Inch'on, South Korea, the first week of December 1951, and then moved into combat in the mountains of North Korea overlooking the Yokkuk-ch'on River valley, west of Ch'orwan, North Korea.

Almost immediately after landing in Korea, several new soldiers were assigned to the unit, boosting the company's strength to about 10 percent above typical authorized level. Through a unique set of circumstances, one of those newly assigned soldiers was an experienced noncommissioned officer and a veteran of World War II.

Master Sergeant George F. McCorkle, who hailed from the Keystone state of Pennsylvania, was among the newly arrived soldiers in Korea who had been with the 1st Cavalry Division only a few days and was reassigned to the

45$^{th}$ Infantry Division as our unit moved into the positions held by the 1st Cavalry Division.

This was a talented professional soldier, experienced both as an officer and as a noncommissioned officer, and, as such, he was a valuable aide to the company commander and to me.

He became a close personal friend and advisor.

Shortly before Christmas 1951, George McCorkle gave me a small devotional book that had been mailed to him by the Brandywine Manor Sunday School class of a church in his hometown in Pennsylvania. The book had been sent as a Christmas gift from that community to its soldiers serving overseas. The book was small enough that it could be easily carried in a field jacket pocket or pack. The book contained brief one-page devotional messages and appropriate Bible verses—one page for each day during a year.

My new friend was of the Catholic faith and for some reason did not want to use the devotional guide. He felt I would enjoy the book. That seemingly insignificant act impacted my life and my worship experiences while in Korea and for all the years since then. I used that devotional book during those days of war and have read through the book time and again for periods of daily devotional experiences during the more than half-century that has passed since 1951.

The book became a treasured possession—a reminder of a friend from long ago and a time of long ago. During the more than half-century since that small devotional book was given to me, I have retained it for almost daily reading. The pages are frayed and slightly yellowed. The cover is worn. The words read each day remind me of God's love, forgiveness, guidance and protection.

The book was especially important during those challenging months in Korea.

Here are some words that I read one of those days more than a half-century ago while sitting in a bunker in the snow-covered ground in below-zero degrees weather and with an enemy just a short distance away.

---

*February Third*

"*Yea, though I walk through the valley of the shadow death, I will fear no evil: for thou art with me; thy rod and thy staff they comfort me.*"
— *Psalm 23:4*

*THE valley of the shadow of death" may refer to any dark, dread or awful experience through which the child of God may be called upon to pass-sorrow, affliction, bereavement, poverty, persecution, death.*

*It is kind of our Great Shepherd that He permits the valley to come in the middle of the Psalm and not at the beginning; after we have been in green pastures of fellowship with Him and are strengthened for conflict.*

*O, the thoughtfulness of God in our behalf.*

*The valley of the shadow of death is very narrow. We pass through it in single file. No earthly friend can go with us in death. So we note that the personal pronoun is changed from "he" to "thou," from third to second.*

*But if you have Christ as Savior and Shepherd you can say: "Though I walk through the valley of the shadow of death I will fear no evil for thou art with me; thy rod and thy staff they comfort me.*"

*Rev. William Evans, D.D., Ph.D.*
*Los Angeles. California*

---

These words remain true for all of us in the current days of uncertainty.

The devotional book, "God's Message," was treasured during the days in Korea and for six decades following the war.

*Soldiers of the 45th Infantry Division built the Christian Church in Chitose, Japan, on Hokkaido Island. Money for the materials to build the church was collected for several weeks in chapel services. The church building was finished in November 1951 just a few days before the 180th Infantry Regimental Combat Team departed Hokkaido for duty in Korea. The new church was built in the center of Chitose, near the Chitose River, a beautiful stream that had been enjoyed by many of us from Company C and other units during off-duty time visits into the nearby town.*

*(Archives, 45th Infantry Division Museum)*

*Captain Ralph A. Purdy (above) of New Orleans, Louisiana was chaplain for the 180$^{th}$ Infantry Regiment and became the pastor of a strange and mixed flock of soldiers who were of many denominations and some who were of no denomination.*

*Company Clerk Corporal Donald Peterson, Sioux Falls, South Dakota, was a high school music teacher before he was drafted into service. He had a perfect tenor voice and volunteered to lead singing for chapel services.*

*Master Sergeant George F. McCorkle (left) of Coatesville, Pennsylvania, and Master Sergeant Clarence G. Oliver, Jr. in front of Company C's command post tent.*

*(March 1952)*

*Christians and War—*

A Christian who is serving in the military, most certainly one who is in a combat unit, at some point must come to grips with and find answers to some serious religious questions, including this one:

"Can a person be both a combat soldier and a Christian?"

Finding the answer to that question is a deeply personal matter.

I do not recall ever having serious doubts about whether I could be a soldier and a Christian. My belief undoubtedly was influenced by church experiences as a young teen during the World War II years when millions of the nation's men and women were serving in military units around the world and when most church services included a time of special prayer for all those who were in uniform and "in harm's way."

Many of our relatives, neighbors and friends were among those whose names were lifted up in prayer at home and in church services. Their lives, their faith and their Christian service, as well as their heroic actions in war, were recalled and praised.

No one in those services gave any thought to questioning the "Christian beliefs" of those brave young men and women.

The Bible—throughout the Old Testament—is filled with examples of God instructing his chosen people, the Israelites, to make war against neighboring nations where pagan gods were worshiped and the people who were considered enemies. Since God ordered those wars, there is a logical assumption that God must approve of military service.

Those were Old Testament days, though, before Jesus Christ's birth, life, ministry, death, resurrection and ascension to Heaven.

Also, those events related to God's chosen race of people.

Was it reasonable for those of us in modern times to assume that what God condoned for the Israelites many centuries ago also applied to us, those who had chosen to believe in Jesus Christ as God's son who was sent to the world to save us humans?

That was a serious question to ponder.

We who had professed belief in Christ as the Savior had indicated through that action that we intended to follow his teachings and example of love, kindness, helpfulness and concern for others.

How did being a modern day Christian conform to being a soldier, sailor, marine or airman who in performing his or her military duty might be called upon to kill or harm other humans?

Would that military service be acceptable to our Lord?

Finding the answers to those questions called for searching the New Testament writings, especially the Gospels and the history of the early church, to study about the lives and activities of the early-day Christians and to determine what, if anything, Jesus had to say about Christianity and military service.

Interestingly, several stories were found in which Jesus had interaction with soldiers.

God has his own plan for things. His ways are not man's ways.

Evidence of that fact is that God apparently chose a soldier to be the first Gentile to be converted to be a follower of Christ. I had known the story from the New Testament book of history, *The Acts of the Apostles,* about how God used a vision to lead the Apostle Peter to the home of

Cornelius, who was a Roman Centurion, a commander of a company of Roman soldiers.

In that book is recorded the story about an angel that appeared to Cornelius and said, "Your prayers and gifts to the poor have come up as a remembrance before God," and he was instructed to send men to Joppa to find Peter and bring him to meet Cornelius.[18]

As the result of that visit, Cornelius, and then through his witness and influence, his entire household became Christians.

There isn't any record that God criticized Cornelius for being a soldier or indicated that he would need to cease being a soldier in order to be a follower of Jesus.

The historian-physician Luke, the writer of both the *Gospel of Luke* and the book of *The Acts of the Apostles,* did an extensive study of Christ's life and teachings. He described that research with these words: "Therefore, since I myself have carefully investigated everything from the beginning, it seemed good also to me to write an orderly account for you, most excellent Theophilus, so that you may know the certainty of the things you have been taught."[19]

Luke, in writing about Cornelius, reported that God looked at Cornelius' heart and saw that this Centurion was "devout and God-fearing" and that "he gave generously to those in need and prayed to God regularly."[20]

God valued this soldier. He was devout and God-fearing. His heart was right.


In the writings of the Apostle Matthew, there is a story of another Roman Centurion who had an encounter with Jesus. The Roman military leader met Jesus and told

---

[18] Acts 10:1-48

[19] Luke 1:3-4

[20] Acts 10:2

him that he had a servant who was paralyzed. He asked Jesus to heal him.

When Jesus said, "I will go and heal him," the Centurion demonstrated his faith when he said, "Lord, I do not deserve to have you come under my roof. But just say the word, and my servant will be healed. For I myself am a man under authority, with soldiers under me. I tell this one, 'Go,' and he goes; and that one, 'Come,' and he comes. I say to my servant, 'Do this,' and he does it."[21]

Matthew, the writer of the story, indicated that Jesus was "astonished" at the Centurion's words.

This Roman understood authority and knew that Jesus had ultimate authority.

Jesus responded to the Centurion and advised all who listened, "I tell you the truth, I have not found anyone in Israel with such great faith." So Jesus said, "Go! It will be done just as you believed it would." And the servant was healed "that very hour."

In dealing with this soldier, Jesus looked at him in the same manner as all others who came to him. He saw the soldier's great faith and he recognized the Centurion's humbleness. Jesus did not condemn the Centurion and say that being a soldier was unacceptable. He did not ask that the Centurion change careers. He said, "I tell you the truth, I have not found anyone in Israel with such great faith."[22]


The question of whether a person can be both a Christian and a soldier was resolved in my mind.

These and other Biblical teachings helped me realize that Christians who are in military service, in the same manner as all Christians, need to have a great commitment

---

[21] Matthew 8:5-13

[22] Acts 8:10

to Jesus Christ and to strive to be as much like Him as possible!

I was convinced that Jesus is in the business of loving and forgiving people, not condemning us.

The most serious discussion with another soldier on this matter came a few years after my return from Korea. This was during a time when I was stationed at Fort Benning, Georgia, studying to improve my military skills in an officers' class at the United States Army Infantry School. The officer, a classmate in the course, and his wife were visiting with my wife and me during a social event at the post.

The officer, also a First Lieutenant in an Infantry unit, had several years of military service but had not been in combat. He and his wife were both Christians. During the visit that evening, the officer asked about my days in Korea and my "feelings" concerning being a Christian and a soldier in wartime.

That was serious talk for two young couples at an evening social event.

A point of discussion focused on the much-debated meaning of the words "You shall not kill," and whether that commandment applies to people in wartime situations.

Based on my earlier study of the questions about a Christian serving in the military, I was convinced that a more accurate translation of the commandment was "You shall not murder," and that the Hebrew word used in the commandment literally referred to the intentional, premeditated killing of another person.

Not being a scholar of the Hebrew language, I had to depend on the knowledge of others in arriving at that belief. I remain convinced that such is the meaning of the commandment, especially since the Old Testament writings told of the many instances when God ordered the Israelites to go to war with other nations. Also, there were the Old Testament stories about how the Jewish people had been directed to follow laws that called for the death penalty for numerous crimes against people.

War is never a good thing, but sometimes it is a necessary action. In a world filled with sinful people, sometimes the only way to keep evil people from doing great harm to others is by going to war with them.

Those were the thoughts shared that night with another soldier and his wife. I had resolved the possible dilemma and no longer struggled with the question of whether one can be both a Christian and a soldier.

One of the oft-repeated statements made about people in war is, "There are no atheists in foxholes."

I don't know who first voiced that opinion. Whether the observation is totally accurate may never be known since the faith experience is very personal and not recorded—except in Heaven.

But, I am convinced that most people who have been thrust into the danger and death associated with combat have become closer to God. I had placed my faith in Christ. Whether in the wartime days in Korea or in the days that followed, these words written by a great soldier and king have given me strength, confidence and comfort:

*"You will not fear the terror of night, nor the arrow that flies by day, nor the pestilence that stalks in the darkness, nor the plague that destroys at midday. A thousand may fall at your side, ten thousand at your right hand, but it will not come near you."*

— *Psalm 91:5-7*

# Chapter Fifteen

## Shot at and Missed—

Long before he was prime minister of Great Britain during the perilous World War II years, Winston Churchill, while serving as a young lieutenant in the British Army in India, penned some words to describe something that many soldiers have felt—the sensation of being "shot at and missed."

The meaning of that phrase really registered with me in February 1952 on a hill overlooking a valley near a much fought-over and unusual piece of terrain known to soldiers then and later as T-Bone Hill.

Churchill was a Second Lieutenant serving with the 4th Queen's Hussar Regiment in India in and near Bangalore, South India, for almost three years during 1896 to 1899. But, he spent time elsewhere as well, notably in India's northwest frontier province of what is now Pakistan. It was from that land that he wrote about his unusual experience.

Churchill's popular dispatches from the frontier described sounds and scenes that have been repeated in many wars, and seemed especially accurate descriptions for those of us who were engaged in combat on the hills and in the valleys of the Korean peninsula.

The young officer who many years later became Prime Minister of England once wrote, "The noise of firing echoed among the hills. Its echoes are ringing still. One valley caught the waves of sound and passed them to the next, till the whole wide mountain region rocked with the confusion of the tumult."

The unique characteristic sound of a bullet or projectile passing nearby is especially memorable. Churchill described that sound with these words: "The bullets passed in the air with a curious sucking noise, like that produced by drawing the air between the lips."[23]

"Nothing in life is so exhilarating as to be shot at without result," Second Lieutenant Winston Churchill of the 4th Queen's Hussar Regiment wrote in describing that experience.

That is precisely the sound—"a curious sucking noise." It is a sound, once heard, is never forgotten.

My most memorable experience of hearing that distinctive sound came when I wanted to take a photograph of a valley near the odd-shaped T-Bone Hill.

That desire for a "good picture" almost cost me my life.

The day, although cold, held forth the hope that spring would soon come to Korea. The sky was partially cloudy. The sun was still edging its way into space above the northern hemisphere.

The Company Command Post, where I spent the major part of each day, was tucked safely into a protected space at the base of the reverse slope of Hill 334. One of Company C's rifle platoons manned positions just on the

---

[23] Churchill (1898), Chapter X

forward slope of the hill, with other platoons stretched out in both directions along fingers of the hill that pointed to T-Bone Hill.

Elements of the 180th Infantry's Heavy Tank Company were mixed in with the infantry unit positions along the MLR to provide direct fire against enemy positions, and to provide supporting fire in the event of an enemy attack against outposts or the occupied space. The tank units also were available to be called on for combined infantry-tank attack assignments for operations against the Chinese held positions when offensive attacks were ordered.

The mountains, hills and narrow valleys of the Korean peninsula did not make for good "tank country." The heavy tanks had to be carefully routed along narrow valley passages and had to avoid the old rice patties that were located in many river valleys.

Getting a tank to the top of a steep hill was a challenge. Somehow, a talented commander and driver from the 180th Tank Company had maneuvered a M4A3 Sherman tank up the hill and along the ridge held by Company C, and into an assigned strategic position that overlooked a wide valley and within firing distance of a range of hills occupied by Chinese army units

The Sherman was a workhorse of a tank. This tank was the mainstay of U.S. armor during World War II and continued to be so during the Korean War. This 37-ton monster was 24 feet long, almost 10-feet wide, and had a 76mm main gun, two 30-caliber machine guns, and a 50-caliber antiaircraft machine gun on top the turret. A crew of five manned the tank.

Having such a powerful bodyguard nearby provided some comfort to the dug-in infantrymen.

But, since both the American and Chinese armies were using "dug-in" tanks in the direct fire-supporting role, the location of a tank at times could also attract enemy fire.

The Sherman tank's 76mm main canon could hurl a variety of shells to targets almost a mile away. This was a powerful weapon. Across the valley, though, were enemy tanks that were being used in a similar manner.

The Chinese army units most likely were equipped with the Russian-built T-34 tanks that were about the same size as the Sherman tank, but with a slightly larger main gun, an 85mm canon with slightly longer range than the 76mm gun on the Sherman tank.

Using a tank gun to launch pinpoint sniper fire at specific targets was an effective tactic. Being on the target side of such a sniper shot was scary.

The tank commander who had been designated to provide supporting fire for Company C's sector had maneuvered the Sherman tank into an area that permitted the tank to be on top the ridge to provide the most effective direct fire, but, when necessary, where the tank could be withdrawn slightly behind the ridgeline and still be able to provide some fire support from a more concealed position.


In the military scheme of things, especially for large-scale offensive operations, battle tactics called for armor and infantry to be employed as a team in battle. Infantrymen and tanks provide mutual support and protection. Tanks without accompanying infantry are vulnerable to enemy tank-killer weapons. Infantry units, without accompanying tanks, are vulnerable to small arms, machineguns and other direct-fire weapons.

Armor offensive tactics also envision armor employed in large formations, moving en masse to overwhelm an enemy and make deep penetrations, as occurred during World War II in the campaigns in North Africa and throughout Western Europe.

But, Korea was not ideal "tank country."

In Korea, tanks were rarely used in large-scale armor-infantry operations, especially during these days after the war stalled and the Army units spent most of the time in holding positions and conducting patrols, skirmishes, and minor clashes along the MLR.

The mountainous terrain and narrow valleys of Korea made it difficult to employ more than a few tanks in one location.

Attempts to employ tanks in larger concentrations invariably led to a number of the tanks becoming bogged down. Even on some smaller attack operations involving two or three tanks in support of an infantry unit attack, the tanks sometimes bogged down in the snow-covered areas in the deep valleys. Retrieving bogged-down or damaged tanks in the valleys that were easily within range of the Chinese weapons was a dangerous activity.

Combined infantry-armor attacks were conducted for some operations, but on a smaller basis and with limited success.

As the result, tanks were often employed for long-range, pinpoint sniping fire against enemy positions. This modified use of tanks proved to be very effective. That was how the Sherman tank that I stood near was being used.

In the hills across the way, a Chinese gun crew was practicing a similar tactic.

The thought of being caught in the crosshairs of the magnifying scope of a Chinese tank gunner who was aiming an 85mm gun for sniper fire is a bit bizarre. That possibility had not crossed my mind as I climbed the hill to check on some friends who were occupying foxholes, a trench and bunkers on the forward slope of the hill just above the Company CP.


During the months prior to my call to active military duty, I had been busy with work as a professional photographer, a job for which I began training immediately after completing high school when I became an apprentice to a professional commercial photographer. Those years were followed by college preparation in journalism, additional work in commercial photography, some brief newspaper photography work, and a brief stint as a free-lance photographer with my own shop before the start of the Korean War and the call to active duty of my unit.

I began that journey of work and study immediately after graduating from high school in Ada, Oklahoma. The new job was viewed as a means of learning about photography—something I hoped would assist me in my planned career as a journalist.

My long-time interest in photography was developed while using the simplest of cameras—the family-owned folding-bellows Kodak, a small Brownie camera and an inexpensive Argos camera that I was able to purchase from earnings from my work as a drug sore soda jerk. Time in the Ada City Library, with access to books and magazines devoted to photography, provided me with photography basics.

I wanted to learn more, though, and was excited when one of the city's finest photographers offered me the opportunity to study the "art and science" of photography as an apprentice in his studio. The pay would be minimal—just $7 per week. The real benefit, though, was the opportunity to learn through one-on-one instruction from a master photographer who would teach me all about photography.

James Stansel, with training in the New York Institute of Photography and years of experience in portrait and commercial photography, owned and operated a Main Street studio that specialized in portrait and commercial photography, as well as wedding photography and other group projects. His work was of exceptional quality, reflecting his superior training and extensive experience.

Although part of my day was spent in handling routine film development and printing, Mr. Stansel spent time each day instructing me on the finer points of photography, beginning with an introduction to his large collections of cameras, ranging from a large 8" x 10" sheet film camera for commercial projects, studio cameras, including a 5" x 7" sheet film portrait camera, high speed press cameras, such as the Speed Graphic that featured a $1/1000^{th}$ second rolling shutter, and smaller roll film cameras that used a variety of film sizes from 120mm, 620mm, 127mm and 35mm varieties.

The instruction moved to darkroom procedures from mixing chemicals, temperature control, various steps in the development and printing process, the use of photo enlargers, contact printers, film and print drying and finishing processes, selection of grades of photo paper, and the very delicate process of retouching negatives to remove slight blemishes on negatives, or to enhance the finished products.

The first summer was a tremendous learning process, and by early fall, after I began my first year of college at East Central State College (later East Central University), I was introduced to the techniques of portrait photography—lighting, sets, backgrounds and steps to help the "subject" be a little more at ease in order to insure a great portrait.

Commercial photography training was next on the agenda. Photographs used for publicity, exhibits, advertising, and other such purposes mostly were of buildings, furniture, equipment, interior and exterior photographs—of things rather than people.

Because of that extensive training, looking for and taking both planned and candid photographs had become second nature to me. I was always looking for photo opportunities, not only for a photo record of the days in Korea, but also for possible use in the hometown newspaper, *The Ada Evening News*, for which I occasionally supplied stories

227

and photographs about the activities of one of the two hometown National Guard units on duty in Korea.

Even in this war zone, a camera normally was kept close by, ready for candid photographs.

On this soon to be memorable day, my interest in photography almost proved deadly.

I tucked my 35mm Argus C-3 camera into a pocket of my field jacket before I left the CP, thinking that I might take some photos of the valley and hills beyond.

Once at the top of the hill, I cautiously moved from position to position to check on members of the rifle platoon that was spread in defensive positions along that sector, and then stopped near the Sherman tank to observe the tank crew's action in firing at selected targets across the valley. The tank commander scanned the Chinese-held territory through powerful binoculars and occasionally directed fire at selected targets.

On that particular day in February 1952, in the sector where Company C was deployed, not much action was taking place. The Chinese had been firing occasional artillery rounds into the area. Once in a while an incoming 120mm mortar round landed, but those were mostly harassing shots, apparently randomly fired toward our positions. The Chinese army units simply wanted to be sure that "our side" knew they were still around.

I pulled my camera from my field jacket pocket and began taking photos of the tank in action, the wide valley and the hills beyond. Then, I turned to take a photo of the area around a fought-over hill that that had come to be known as T-Bone Hill.

During recent days and nights, outpost locations in the valley and on the finger of a ridge leading up the hill seemed to change "ownership" almost daily, with Company

C troops taking possession by day and pulling out during the night when Chinese troops probed those positions.

With the exception of the few rounds fired by the Sherman tank crew, things were rather quiet all along this sector of the MLR. I continued to snap photos and then stood to take a photograph that would capture both the friendly positions along the forward slope of the hill, as well as the Chinese held hills in the distance and the valley in between.

Some of my earlier training as a photographer caused me to work toward properly "framing" a picture, adding depth to the image by including a nearby tree branch in the forefront of the photograph.

In the interest of being a photographer, that day I forgot some of my training as an Infantry soldier.

The result was almost disastrous.

I stood on the ridgeline and moved around a bit in an effort to get into a better position for the desired photograph. Just as I snapped the carefully "framed" picture, I was startled by the sound of a high velocity shell passing just inches above my head, and the "curious," and in this case very loud, "sucking noise" that the young Lieutenant Churchill had once described. My heavy steel helmet was partially lifted off my head by the vacuum created by the passing shell that instantly struck a hillside immediately behind where I was standing, exploding and spewing white phosphorus chemical on the trees and undergrowth and igniting a small fire.

I instantly flattened myself on the ground, waiting for another shot. None came.

I had been "shot at and missed."

Churchill wrote that he found the sound to be "exhilarating."

Perhaps that was true for him. Not for me. I hunkered down—one scared guy.

*A view of valley near T-Bone Hill. Taking this photograph turned out to be an unwise decision by Master Sergeant Clarence G. Oliver, Jr. While he was standing to take the photo, a Chinese-fired tank shell narrowly-missed him. Below, a Sherman tank from the 180th Infantry Regiment Tank Company fires from defensive position on the MLR.          (February 1952)*

Chinese positions across the valley are pounded by direct fire from tanks supporting Company C. Enemy troops fired white phosphorous (WP) 120mm mortar rounds over the protecting hills into company positions on the reverse sides. Soldiers and Korean (KSC) troops are pictured below fighting fires caused by the WP rounds.

# Chapter Sixteen

## Thoughts of Home—

Love knows neither geographic boundaries nor distance.

Thoughts of home, most certainly of my wife and young son, were never very far out of my mind during the days and nights in Korea—especially at night.

A calming of mind and body came over me when I looked into the nighttime sky, sometimes when the moon was visible, and as I talked silently to my wife who was thousands of miles away and obviously could not hear my words.

I could imagine that she did the same.

Much of those moments of quiet time alone were spent praying for her and our son and asking that somehow God would let her have some sense that such thoughts were present with her at that very minute.

I was thankful for my wife and tried to express those thoughts with letters long and short.

Vinita and I had married a few days after our National Guard unit was called to active duty and just three weeks before the unit was to report to Camp Polk, Louisiana. The start of the war in Korea on June 25, 1950, was followed in early July with the notice that the 45th Infantry Division was called to active duty with orders to be in Louisiana on September 1, 1950.

The National Guard units across Oklahoma began making preparations for a quick shift from peacetime duty as part-time civilian soldiers to wartime duty as an active duty military unit. The hometown armory became a beehive of activity.

Normal life and plans changed immediately.

Vinita and I had become engaged six months earlier, on New Year's Eve. Plans had been made to be married the following December at a time I would be approaching the completion of my college education at Oklahoma A&M College—in the future to become Oklahoma State University. Later, Vinita and I decided to move the wedding date to September 1. Plans were made. Invitations were printed. The church was reserved, and Pastor Jack Carroll, for whom Vinita was working as secretary, had the wedding date on his calendar.

The start of the war—and President Harry Truman's decision to "call up" the "Thunderbird" Division—suddenly changed all those plans.

The day Vinita and I picked up the just-printed wedding invitations from the printing shop was the day that we learned that our National Guard unit would report to Louisiana on September 1—our planned wedding day.

What to do?

Some suggested that it might be wise for us to postpone our marriage plans, perhaps even until after the war—a very uncertain date. Vinita and I did not give serious thought to that idea.

A new wedding date was selected. The newly printed wedding invitations were amended as the two of us scratched through the September 1 date, and with pen and ink entries advised all the family and friends that August 7, 1950, was the planned date of our wedding.

The big day was one week away.

Somehow, Vinita's mother, Sally, probably working around the clock at her foot-pedal driven Singer sewing machine, managed to complete a beautiful wedding dress, three dresses for the maid of honor and bridesmaids, make the arrangements for a reception and other related matters—and still ran a household with her usual efficiency.

Vinita and I were married at Oak Avenue Baptist Church in Ada; the church both of us had attended throughout our teenage years. Family members and friends from near and far filled the church to capacity. Thus began our life together.

This was a marriage that I am convinced was "made in Heaven."

Six months later I was on a ship headed to Japan and later to Korea.

The question, "Will I ever see my wife again in this life?" often was on my mind. She and I were now half a world apart—linked only with thoughts, letters and occasional photographs.

Memories of specific events together were recalled again and again—a picnic in the pine tree forests of central Louisiana, a late February drive to the Gulf coast and a barefoot walk in the sand and cold surf, a coveted day trip to Lake Charles for a dinner and movie, and even the special time of sitting in our 1948 Plymouth coupe with the radio softly playing some of the favorite songs of that time, many that became long-standing classics.

One of those 1950's favorites was a somewhat off-beat ballad, "Mona Lisa." That song soared to the top of the music charts and stayed there for weeks. Nat King Cole's mellow delivery of that song contrasted with the singing offered by other popular singers of the early 1950s such as Eddie Fisher, Johnny Ray, and the young Tony Bennett. Cole's careful enunciation of the lyrics helped convey a song with depth and meaning.

Often, during time alone, I tried to recall the lyrics of the song, remembering how it sounded on the car radio the last night Vinita and I were together in DeRidder, Louisiana, in March 1951, the night before our unit left Camp Polk and shipped out of the Port of New Orleans, headed to the Far East—first to Japan and then to Korea.

The lyrics of the popular song were a reminder of my love, Vinita, back home in Oklahoma.

Even while wrapped in a mountain sleeping bag in the darkness of a cold bunker in Korea I could almost hear the husky voice of Nat King Cole as he sang these words:

*"Mona Lisa, Mona Lisa*
*Men have named you*
*You're so like the lady*
*With the mystic smile.*
*Is it only cause you're lonely*
*They have blamed you?*
*For that Mona Lisa*
*Strangeness in your smile?"*[24]

Another of the hit songs of the times, "Goodnight Irene," also came to mind. That song, too, was played on our car radio that special night.

Vinita did not like the "Goodnight Irene" song, and seemed to groan each time it was played. She said it reminded her of my departure for war. But, for me, it was a reminder of our wonderful days together during our early months of marriage.

---

[24] Lyrics by Jay Livingston and Music by Ray Evans. Copyright 1949, Famous Music Corporation.

235

I liked the song, though, and the tune almost always came to mind when I thought back on those days and nights.

Pete Seeger of the folk group, *The Weavers*, had revived the old American folk standard and made it one of the top hit tunes of the year. Oh how that man could sing that and other folks songs!

In my mind, I could almost hear Seeger's husky voice as he sang the chorus:

*"Goodnight Irene, goodnight*
*Goodnight Irene, goodnight*
*Goodnight Irene, goodnight Irene*
*I'll see you in my dreams."*

The second verse of the revitalized old-time folk song told of a parting of young lovers:

*"One night I got married*
*Now me and my wife settled down*
*Now me and my wife are parting*
*I want to jump overboard in a river and drown."*[25]

The words and the music remained imbedded in my mind—in those days of war, as well as half-a-century later.

Ours was a love that had grown through the years after circumstances brought us together even in our pre-teen years. During those winter nights in Korea I often thought back to the time of our youth and recalled the events that led to our becoming friends, then sweethearts, and then happily married—a journey of eight years.

---

[25] Words and Music by Huddie Ledbetter, Copyright, 1936, 1950, 1964, Ludlow Music Inc.

In the early summer of 1942 when I was 12 years old and soon to be 13, I had moved up the city park system's work ladder from a job of cleaning the children's wading pool for "swimming privileges" to working at the "big pool" at the Glenwood City Park in Ada, Oklahoma. My job became one of handling such major assignments as scrubbing the shower and dressing areas, getting the bathhouse ready for the day's swimmers, plus, at least to me, the impressive job of removing the "cotton" and leaves that fell each day in the water from massive Cottonwood trees that towered over the south end of the pool. Screening the "cotton" was one of the last work items before the gates were opened for the afternoon swimming session.

It was during that summer of 1942 that Vinita June Shirley arrived on the scene. She came to the swimming pool to supervise her two younger brothers, Jerry and Charles, as they swam. And, according to her telling of the story in later years, she observed this dark brown-skinned boy, me, cleaning the pool and couldn't determine if I was an Indian or a Negro youth because my skin was so darkly tanned.

The Shirley family was new to Ada, having moved to the community from Pauls Valley during the final six weeks of the school year. The family lived on West 12th Street, just two blocks from Glenwood Park. Vinita and Jerry had finished the school year at the nearby Glenwood Elementary School, transferring from their school in Pauls Valley and just beginning to get acquainted with their new hometown. Charles, the youngest, had not yet entered school. Vinita was ready to begin the seventh grade the next fall at Ada Junior High School, where I was already a student and getting ready for my eighth grade year.

The Shirley family, for whatever reason, made a decision to make Oak Avenue Baptist Church, located at the corner of North Oak Avenue and West Sixth Street, their new "church home." That decision by Vinita's parents, Arthur Lee and Alva (Sally) Shirley, with their children to become members of that church set in motion a wonderful series of events for the two of us.

Although both of us were attending Ada Junior High School, she in the seventh grade and I in the eighth grade, I really became consciously aware of her presence during our time together in the youth Sunday School department at Oak Avenue Baptist Church.

The Christmas season at church was a special time, particularly with the preparation for and presentation of the annual Christmas Pageant. Although with slightly different themes, music, and acting, the pageant each year always included the traditional nativity scene—usually placing Mary, Joseph and the baby Jesus in a makeshift manger created in the dry baptistery tank—and with the cast of players who assumed the roles of angels, shepherds and kings usually included many of us from the youth department.

Vinita, tall and slender, with long blonde hair and gorgeous hazel eyes, was a regular choice for the angel choir, and, in time, was promoted to the prominent role of the Angel Gabriel.

Each Christmas season, the month-long time of practice sessions to prepare for the annual pageant permitted us to spend a great deal of time together. Friendships were strengthened by the common focus and the good times of togetherness. There was much excitement in the air.

On one specific occasion, a Saturday night final dress rehearsal just one night before the pageant presentation on a Sunday evening, I recall the exact moment when, even as a 16-year-old youth, that I knew that I was really in love and "going to marry" Vinita one day. From that time forth, there was never any doubt in my mind of the goal, although several years would pass before Vinita could be wooed and persuaded.

The precise moment came during time when all of us in the cast were donning costumes and, with the assistance of adult sponsors, using spirit gum to stick itchy false beards to our faces and putting on other make-up which was felt necessary for the forthcoming performance. The make-up activity space was shared by all of us. I remember looking across the small room at Vinita as she sat before a mirror while she applied lipstick and brushed her golden hair—looking every part the role of the angel that she was to portray. She turned her head and those beautiful eyes looked straight at me. Then she turned back to the mirror.

At that moment, I knew that this young lady one day would be my wife—and we had not even had a first date. The year was 1945.

That first date would come a few weeks later as we approached St. Valentine's Day.

I had fallen in love. Vinita didn't know it, but I did. It would be several weeks later before I had the nerve to ask for a date. Her wise father had set forth a requirement that she could not date until she was 16 years old. However, Lee Shirley did relent—by one month—and in February, 1946, with Vinita's acceptance of the invitation, and with her father's agreement since he knew me and could keep an eye on me every Sunday in church, I called on Miss Vinita June Shirley at her home—the first date.

That date consisted of the two of us walking to downtown Ada, a leisurely stroll of nine city blocks, just short of one mile, taking in a movie at the Ritz Theater on East Main Street, enjoying the usual Cokes and popcorn during the movie, and a walk in the moonlight back to her home. I, then, had another walk to my home, another mile north. Since neither family owned a car, walking to every destination was the norm.

Throughout the evening, during the walk to and from downtown Ada, as well as throughout the movie, our hands barely touched. Talk about two bashful teenagers! But, the 1940s for two Depression-era kids was a simpler time.

Our first movie together was a recent Hollywood production, *The Song of Bernadette*. The movie starred a young Oklahoma beauty, Jennifer Jones, who portrayed a young French peasant girl in the late 1850s who had an experience of a vision of the Virgin Mary and who was instructed to dig in the ground, resulting in the discovery of the underground spring of "healing water" that would make the town of Lourdes, France, world-renowned.

That was a pretty serious movie for a couple of teenagers on our first date.

There were to be many movies viewed together in the years to follow, the titles not remembered. That first one together, though, made a lasting impression—not only because of the story, but also because of the start of a wonderful courtship.

During the few months that followed before the end of the school year, we two somewhat bashful teenagers carefully communicated our feelings to each other through notes, cautiously written, neatly folded and carefully passed in a Spanish class, our one shared course, or the occasional passing in the hallways of the three-story brick building which housed Ada High School.

It was springtime, that wonderful season of the year between winter and summer during which the weather becomes warmer and plants revive and boys fall in love.

At least, this boy was in love—hopelessly so.


There are a million memories—mostly good—which are associated with those high school and early college years.

Although both of us, on occasions, dated other people, the two of us invariable were drawn back together—most certainly each spring. Even when not dating regularly, Vinita and I, along with our friends, a group of eight or nine close friends from church and which all of us lovingly described as "the gang," enjoyed time together for social events at church, in family homes, evening drives, picnics, parties, trips to the Kit-Kat drive-in for hamburgers and Cokes, and scores of other activities that are so important to young people.

Whether because of our first date, or the occasion of Vinita's March birthday, or other reasons, spring became a special and very favorite season of the year for both of us.


Four years would pass before two much more mature young people would reach the point of an engagement and discussion of marriage.

Vinita and I often returned from dates or evening events at church and parked my family's aging 1938 model Chevy in the driveway of the Shirley home on West Fourth Street in order to talk or simply be together a little bit longer that evening. Such was the case on a New Year's Eve winter night in 1949 when Vinita said, "Yes," in response to my question, "Will you marry me?"

I was nearing my senior year status at Oklahoma A&M College, located almost 100 miles away in Stillwater. She was a student at East Central State College in Ada and working as the pastor's secretary at Oak Avenue Baptist Church. Vinita was popular at college and at church and one of my great fears was that one of her many other suitors might be successful in persuading her to marry one of them.

To me, that was a very valid concern. I was fearful that the old saying, "Absence makes the heart grow fonder," might not work. She was too important in my life.

Fortunately for me, she agreed to be engaged to be married to me—even though, at that time, there were a lot of unknowns concerning just how I could support a wife and start a family. Surprisingly, neither of us seemed to be concerned about those matters.

We had strong belief in the teaching that "God would direct our steps."

He did.

If ever there was a "match made in heaven," this was such a match.

Such were the thoughts of home that came to my mind even though I was 10,000 miles from home.

*A constant reminder of home and family—of my wife, Vinita, and our young son, Paul—was with me daily in Korea with this small leather photo wallet. The leather became battered and stained, but survived the rain, sleet, snow and dirt.*

# Chapter Seventeen

# War of Words—

The only enemy aircraft to venture over the front line positions during the 1951-1952 winter-spring months were those that made occasional night time flyovers—small airplanes that, for the most part, were on a mission to drop propaganda leaflets.

North Korean or Chinese fighter-bombers and Russian made MIG jet fighter planes—presumed to be flown by Russian pilots—seldom left the North Korean skies after the opening months of the war in Korea. The U. S. Air Force, along with the aircraft carrier based U. S. Navy and Marine Corps air units, controlled the skies in our sector of Korea.

Those infrequent visits by enemy aircraft seemed to be limited to small, older civilian-style airplanes that occasionally flew into the area to drop propaganda leaflets. The sound of the small engine, one that must have been about an 80-90 horsepower variety, was similar to the sound of the Piper Cub airplane engines that most of us remembered from back home.

Some units reported that those small airplanes sometimes dropped mortar shells along the front. To my knowledge, that did not happen in our sector.

The enemy visitors in the air were given the name of "Bed Check Charlie" because they usually flew in and out of the area about bedtime.

Such visits were rare. Evidence of the visits consisted of propaganda leaflets that were found scattered across the front.

The North Korean and Chinese propaganda material more frequently was delivered by enemy mortar and artillery shells designed to burst open in the air and with the wind scattering the contents of pamphlets. Others were left in front of the lines by enemy patrols or intruders, with the propaganda left along trails or in areas in which our own patrols were likely to move.

Both sides practiced the war of words and pictures— using paper as the propaganda weapon. Millions of pamphlets, letters, safe conduct passes and pleas to troops were used in attempts to influence the thoughts of the soldiers along the front lines.

The propaganda efforts of the Chinese and North Koreans were attempts to introduce dissent or apathy among soldiers. The pamphlets, flyers and other material sometimes got passed around among soldiers in Company C, but didn't seem to have any impact—or, none that I could detect. Just how much the propaganda prepared by the United States and other allies and aimed at the North Koreans and Chinese had any impact on those forces was difficult to know.

The first Chinese prisoner captured after the 180th Infantry Regimental Combat Team moved into combat positions may have been, in part, the result of the U.S. propaganda promises of safe conduct, hot food and warm clothing. The prisoner of war was captured near a Company C outpost.

Sergeant David E. Monroe of Birmingham, Alabama, who was leading a small team that occupied an outpost located forward of Company C's positions, was credited with capturing the 45th Division's first prisoner of war—without a struggle. Just as Sergeant Monroe stepped outside an outpost bunker, he saw a Chinese soldier standing a few feet away from the outpost. He yelled at the soldier, who instantly raised his hands above his head in surrender.

While the other three soldiers watched carefully to see if more Chinese soldiers might be nearby and kept rifles aimed at the new prisoner, Sergeant Monroe searched the prisoner for weapons and information. Nothing unusual was found on the soldier, who was then taken under guard to the Regimental headquarters for interrogation.

The Chinese soldier told interpreters that he surrendered because food was scarce in the Communist armies and that many of the enlisted men in his unit were dissatisfied with the war.

The other men who manned the combat outpost and shared in the capture were Private First Class Gerald Davis of Kirbyville, Texas; Private First Class William Putt of Fort Wayne, Indiana, and Private First Class James Kerwood of Sattas, West Virginia.[26]


A lot of thought and planning went into the preparation of the propaganda. As an example, one U.S. leaflet that was aimed at the Chinese and North Korean soldiers contained a cartoon that depicted Soviet leader Joseph Stalin pushing a Chinese officer who was pushing a Korean sol-

---

[26] *The 45th Division News*, December 1951, Archives, 45th Infantry Division Museum.

dier toward a battlefield named "Korea." The flyer suggested that the Russians were driving the Korean War.

The propaganda leaflets were designed to cause doubt, to make soldiers question why they were risking their lives in a foreign civil war while their family and loved ones waited for them at home. The propaganda drops often were timed to coincide with special holidays such as Christmas, New Years' Eve or Easter in an attempt to make soldiers feel homesick.

The desire to be home with family was present with soldiers most of the time. Whether it could be called "homesickness" was questionable. Wanting to be home was normal.

Although none of the propaganda leaflets tempted us to take advantage of the "Safe Conduct" pass offers, a couple of the flyers did cause me to think about family and home—even a bit more than normal. One such leaflet featured a Norman Rockwell-like picture of an American family gathered for a holiday meal, while on the other side was a snow-covered American soldier in frozen North Korea.

The message said,

*"Frozen Rations eaten on the run. Any moment he may have to run again, to fight or die—and so may you. Those who love you want you back home safe and sound. FIND A WAY OUT! It's no disgrace to quit fighting in this unjust war!"*

Did the propaganda persuade some to defect—to reject this country and to run to the enemy for whatever reason?

Perhaps a few soldiers believed the deceptive messages, but none from our unit walked away.

Approximately 1.5 million U. S. soldiers served in Korea during the three years of war. Records indicate that 7,140 American soldiers were captured and interned during the war. Of that number, 2,701 died while in Prisoner of War camps, 4,418 were returned to the United States. Only 21 of those prisoners refused repatriation, accepting the social-political Communist brainwashing.

The status of another approximately 2,000 soldiers remained a mystery at the end of the war. They were listed missing in action (MIA) and presumed dead—or otherwise unaccounted-for in military records. A few may have "crossed-over" and disappeared into a Communist society. Most likely, though, those MIA soldiers died and lie in unmarked graves somewhere in Korea.[27]

The Chinese and North Korean propaganda pamphlets were interesting to look at and read. A few were collected as souvenirs of the war. The rest simply disappeared in the wind and snow of the Korean mountains—ineffective in the attempt to persuade American soldiers to give up the fight.

The Chinese and North Korean propaganda leaflets often emphasized solidarity among all soldiers. Most of the propaganda portrayed soldiers from the United States and other United Nations military units as simple pawns in a game played by rich businessmen who were said to be profiting from the war.

Ours was a proud unit with soldiers who had great self-respect and a love for our nation that God had so richly blessed. None of us was about to do something that would disgrace the United States.

---

[27] Cole (1994), xv-xvi

This Christmas season propaganda leaflet made soldiers think
of home. The text reads: "Frozen Rations eaten on the run.
Any moment he may have to run again, to fight or die—and
so may you. Those who love you want you back home safe and
sound. FIND A WAY OUT! It's no disgrace to quit fighting
in this unjust war!"
(Archives, 45th Infantry Division Museum)

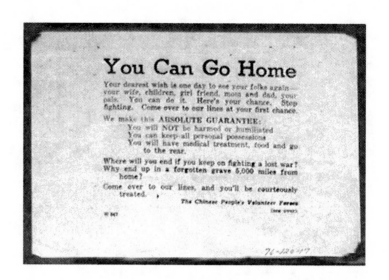

*Both sides issued various "Safe Conduct" passes during the war to encourage soldiers to surrender. The photo (below) shows UN prisoners being well treated. The words, "Demand peace, Stop the war," were often used in North Korean-Chinese propaganda flyers to imply that the war was unwanted by all soldiers.*
*(Archives, 45ᵗʰ Infantry Division Museum)*

The "Mr. Moneybags" propaganda pamphlet aimed at U.S.
troops appeared frequently in December. The top picture was
in color, and the text reads: "Mr. Moneybags in Florida this
Christmas." The black and white picture of soldiers had the
text, "Where are you? In Korea! You risk your life; big business rakes in the dough."
(Archives, 45ᵗʰ Infantry Division Museum)

*United Nations propaganda leaflets targeted both enemy soldiers and Korean civilians. One leaflet was aimed at North Korean and Chinese soldiers, with a cartoon depicting Soviet leader Joseph Stalin pushing a Chinese officer pushing a Korean soldier towards a battlefield named "Korea". It suggested that the Korean War was being driven by the Soviets.*

*Propaganda was also used to show that United Nations forces were working towards uniting Korea, while North Korean forces were under the control of outside forces—the Soviet Union and China.*

*(Archives, 45<sup>th</sup> Infantry Division Museum)*

Although the North Koreans and Chinese lacked the resources to match the propaganda disseminations of the United Nations, they attached great importance to every form of propaganda. Considerable numbers of leaflets were disseminated on the Korean battlefields. Many of the leaflets were distributed by mortar fire and by night patrols that simply threw them into advanced positions. One unique Christmas season item was this "Peace" handkerchief. The message on the border read: "From the Chinese Peoples Volunteers in Korea, 1951. Demand Peace. Stop the War. It's no disgrace to quit fighting in this unjust war. Withdraw all foreign troops from Korea; leave Korea to the Koreans."

*(Archives, 45th Infantry Division Museum)*

# Chapter Eighteen

## Everything Isn't Black and White—

The war in Korea wasn't the only conflict in which the United States was engaged during those challenging years of the early 1950s. Some social and political issues also were ongoing at the time. They, too, had impact on those of us serving in the military.

For those of us in Korea, the enemy was known and usually was within eyesight, or, at the very least, his hiding places were known. Combat, or the constant potential for armed battle, was something those of us in that far-off land knew all too well. The other conflicts were not so clearly defined.

While the fighting continued up and down the peninsula nation of Korea, the Army, as well as the entire nation, was involved in two additional major conflicts—the international political battle that became known as the Cold War and the internal social struggle that had dogged the nation since before the War Between the States or the Civil War—that of racial segregation.

Each of the conflicts was unique.

255

Although vastly different from the "shooting war" in Korea, the other conflicts were real and would involve those of us fighting in Korea in ways most of us did not anticipate.

While the "real war" in Korea was being fought in the traditional sense of combat, there was another type of conflict taking place in Europe and other parts of the world where Communism, usually thought of as led by the Union of Soviet Socialist Republics (USSR), was being forced on people and nations through political, social, economic and military action.

The USSR, once an ally of sorts during World War II, was now a new type of enemy, armed and threatening, but not in front line battles with the countries of the "free world." The leaders of that nation apparently were involved in the planning and providing support of the war being fought in Korea, but only in the background—not with troops in the front lines.

The other conflict, with its social and political implications, was the effort to desegregate the nation, including the armed forces. Just how that effort worked at the lowest level, here in a frontline infantry company engaged in battle, was interesting.

Almost 90 years earlier during the middle of the Civil War years President Abraham Lincoln had issued the Emancipation Proclamation that was interpreted as "freeing" slaves in the states that were then in the Confederacy. In reality, though, the practice of imposing the social separation of races had continued, and the resulting discrimination against people of color remained in much of America's society—including in the United States Army that maintained segregated military units.

Two years prior to the start of the Korean War, President Harry S Truman issued an executive order that called for "equality of treatment and opportunity for all persons in the armed services without regard to race, color, religion, or national origin." In addition, a Presidential committee was established to develop the plan to eliminate segregated military units in the United States.[28]

In the midst of the Korean War, that committee concluded that military efficiency would be improved with full utilization of Negro troops in totally integrated military units.

Making a plan was one thing. Making the plan work was an entirely different matter.

The new military policy did not eliminate the all-black fighting units in the Army during the Korean War. Instead, the assignment of Negro soldiers into newly integrated units began by mixing Negro soldiers, including new draftees, into established units, as new replacements were required.

The 45th Infantry Division, recently deployed to front line combat positions in Korea, was one of the units selected for the integration effort.

The first Negro soldiers assigned to our unit climbed out of a truck at the company's headquarters tent late one evening in February 1952 while the 180th Infantry Regiment was in a reserve location being prepared to move once again into a frontline combat assignment.

The five or six young black draftees, all from the northeastern United States, mostly New Jersey, were cold after a long truck ride in sub-freezing weather when they arrived at the Company C location. They most likely were also very scared.

That was easy to understand.


These young soldiers were far from home and knew that they were the first black soldiers to be assigned to what

---

[28] Executive Order 9981, *Federal Register 13 (1948): 4313.*

previously would have been called an "all-white" military unit.

The "all-white" term really was not a very accurate description of the unit. The 45th Infantry Division was an Oklahoma-based National Guard unit that had been called to active duty just a few days after the Korean War began. The original membership of the division—as well as Company C, 180th Infantry Regiment—still accounted for about two-thirds of the unit's total roster.

As was true with many Oklahomans, a significant percentage of the soldiers in Company C were of Indian heritage—to some degree—including several soldiers who were "full blood" Indians. In addition, some of the original draftees who were assigned to Company C in November 1950 when the division began combat training in Camp Polk, Louisiana, also were of Indian heritage—including some Sioux tribal members from the Dakotas.

Also, among the original contingent of draftees from New Jersey, Louisiana and Arkansas, along with one very outgoing young man from Puerto Rico, were men who brought distinct Hispanic and Italian heritages into the mix of soldiers.

The young black soldiers who were joining us that night were being involuntarily "integrated" into the company, and, to them, they were being placed into what they perceived as an "all white" Army unit.

This was to be an unusual experience for them—and others.

Because of my childhood experiences and the fact that my family's home was in an older neighborhood that bordered on the segregated black community in Ada, Oklahoma, I did not hold the same feelings of uneasiness or prejudice of some.

My first real awareness of segregation of races came during a time when I promoted from a neighborhood elementary school at the end of the sixth grade and began my junior high school education in a new school building located in a more affluent part of the city.

While riding a bicycle around the community when I was 11 or 12 years old, I had visited the campus on which both the senior high school and junior high school facilities were located. I knew that the building that had been in use for the junior high school was an aging four-story, red brick building. The building was built shortly after statehood, finished in 1909, and had served as an all-purpose school structure during the early years—the city's combined Southside Grade School and Ada High School.

The old building was showing its age during the 1930s, and in 1939 a new junior high school building was finished. That new building, with its wide hallways, beautiful auditorium and gymnasium, sparkling clean floors, large classrooms, new desks, and all the other amenities of a new school was to be my school home for the next three years.

The old junior high school building was demolished. The salvaged bricks were used in the construction of another new school—but one not quite so elegant. The used bricks went to the new Napier School, built near the fairgrounds north of the city to serve the Negro students of the community.

I don't recall being aware of the concept of "separate schools" until that time. Perhaps I was naive, but I thought that children went to schools in their neighborhoods. Suddenly, now I saw that the separation was not by chance of living in certain neighborhoods but by legal decisions imposed on those of another race.

My parents never expressed any feelings of or about racial prejudice or discrimination that I can recall, so none of those feelings were instilled into my thinking.

Our home was in an older part of the city, an area that was the original town site, and was just four blocks west of the area or the city where most Negro families resided. It was not unusual for children from the entire area—various

259

races—to be together on the playground of the nearby Irving Grade School after school hours, during weekends and summer days.

In addition, at one point in my work as a newspaper carrier, my paper route included the neighborhood, sometimes referred to by people as "the flats," in which Negro families resided.

Whether I was just ignorant or simply naive, I was about 12 years old before some of the conditions of racial inequity really became evident to me. That didn't seem "right" to me; but there wasn't much a 12-year-old boy could do about such social issues.

From time to time during my youth, the thoughts of the "wrongness" would return to me. Those were just passing thoughts, though.

Some of those childhood thoughts returned when I learned that some Negro soldiers were to be assigned to Company C.

As the unit's administrative officer, I was the one who would meet the new replacements, review their personnel files, determine their areas of military specialty, process them into the unit and add them to the company roster.

A soldier's 201 file is a collection of all records for a person. The file typically contains all paperwork created about, for or on behalf of an individual. Included are enlistment records, pay records, training records, sometimes a photo, promotions, awards, recommendations, family information, reprimands, assignment history, skills, any disciplinary action and other related documents.

It is a soldier's life history in the Army.

In order to recommend to the Company Commander some possible platoon and squad assignments for the newly arrived replacements, I made a careful study of the 201 files to check the "MOS's" of each of the newcomers to see if any had any unusual training or experience, and reviewed other vital information in the files. After all, if a well-trained "cook" or "baker" was in the group, then that person could be much more valuable in the unit's mess section than being assigned as a rifleman in an infantry platoon.

The Military Occupational Specialty (MOS) is a job classification system used by the Army to indicate an individual's specific area of training and the skill level achieved by that soldier. There were 200 to 300 different specialties in the Army's MOS system at that time. Several dozen different specialties related to an Infantry rifle company.

During those "brown shoe" Army years, the basic personnel record included the "race" of an individual soldier. The forms offered three options for designation of race: "White," "Negro" and "Other," with space provided to indicate specific racial information to explain the "Other" designation.

As I scanned the 201 files of the new replacements, I noticed that the race of one of the men was shown as "American Indian."

Earlier, as I met the newly assigned soldiers when they reported for duty, I observed that all appeared to be Negro soldiers. Thus, the "American Indian" entry caught my attention. The race of an individual would not have any bearing on his assignment; however, as the unit administrator, insuring the accuracy of the personnel file was my responsibility.

Later in the evening, I asked the soldier whose 201 file indicated he was "American Indian" to come to the headquarters tent for clarification of information. During the unit's temporary location in reserve status, the company headquarters office and the unit supply section were housed in one large squad tent. On duty that evening in the supply section were Sergeant John C. Matthews, the supply sergeant, full-blood Cherokee Indian from Tupelo, Oklahoma, and Corporal Bernard W. Whiting, a supply clerk from St. Francis, South Dakota, a full-blood Sioux Indian.

When the soldier arrived, I told him that I wanted to verify some information in his personnel file, that I noticed that his race was listed as "American Indian," and asked him if the information was correct.

"Yes," that's right," the soldier responded.

I then asked the soldier if he knew that his new unit was a company that was originally from Oklahoma, and that about two-thirds of the people in the unit were native Oklahomans. He didn't know anything about the unit and very little about Oklahoma.

The soldier became a little uneasy when I told him that the state's name, Oklahoma, means "Home of the Red Man" and came from the Choctaw Indian words "okla," meaning people, and "humma" meaning red. Then, I said, "Do you see the two soldiers over in the supply area?"

He glanced at Sergeant Matthews and Corporal Whiting, the two full-blood Indians, one Cherokee and one Sioux.

I explained, "Well, those two soldiers are 'American Indians.'"

Then, when I asked him if all the information in his 201 file was accurate, he said that the personnel clerk in New Jersey must have misunderstood and that the "American Indian" race entry was incorrect.

As I changed the personnel record, making a corrected entry to reflect the soldier's race as "Negro," I felt bad about the discussion, about the embarrassment that I had caused this young man, and about the fact that a long history of acts of discrimination in our nation had caused this young man to attempt to "change his race"—at least on paper.

Suddenly, I felt that by challenging the soldier on this matter I, too, had displayed some subconscious bias that I had always presumed did not exist in my mind—and I was ashamed.

A commitment was made to myself that I would not willingly fall into such a prejudicial trap again.


Many years later, in a peacetime setting in the United States while serving as the commanding officer of another National Guard unit into which I had recruited several black soldiers, I had the opportunity on several occasions to stand up for the rights of those soldiers as the racial prejudices continued to be demonstrated in our land.

The promise made to myself 10 years earlier was kept.


Implementation of the new military policies that followed President Truman's 1948 executive order did not eliminate all-black fighting units in the Korean War, but it paved the way for the inclusion of both white and black soldiers into integrated units by mixing established units with replacements when needed.

That was a slow process, though. By 1954, the last all-black unit had been disbanded and Negro soldiers were accepted without a quota system.

The Korean War was the turning point in the full acceptance of Negro soldiers as proven fighters. The Army eliminated 300 all-black units. There were more than 300,000 African-Americans integrated into previously all-white units when the Korean War ended on July 27, 1953.

*Regardless of location, even "on the move," the Army's paperwork continues. Master Sergeant Clarence G. Oliver, Jr., Company C's administrative officer, types away on a reliable Remington portable typewriter preparing personnel records, daily reports and unit orders.*

# Chapter Nineteen

## Going Home—

The calendar that appeared one day on the inside ceiling wall of the squad tent in which some of the senior noncommissioned officers were housed reflected the month of March 1952, drawn with chalk. The date of March 28 was circled. That was the designated day "rotation" would begin for the first soldiers from Company C to leave Korea for home.

Sergeant First Class Paul N. Scott, the unit supply sergeant, now a veteran of two wars and the elder statesman in the group, was credited with drawing the calendar. He also assumed the daily responsibility of placing a large "X" across the dates on the calendar as the countdown began for the first group of soldiers chosen to "rotate" home— selected to start the months-long process of the original members of the 45th Infantry Division returning to the United States.

We were going home.

What a wonderful thought!

*Sergeant First Class Paul N. Scott, supply sergeant, marked off days on the tent ceiling wall calendar, showing the all-important March 28, 1952, "rotation day."*

*First of Company C's soldiers to head home gathered for a group photo a week before departing the unit. Pictured are (left to right, back row) Sergeant John C. Matthews, Sergeant First Class Paul N. Scott, Sergeant Melvin C. Taylor, Master Sergeant John B. Farnham, Jr.; and (front row), Master Sergeant Clarence G. Oliver, Jr. and Sergeant Billie L. Gray.*

The point system for determining the order of rotation was based on a number of factors, including marriage, children, rank, length of service and date of enlistment. There were six soldiers in Company C who were selected for the first rotation from the unit. In the group were Master Sergeant John B. Farnham, Jr., Sergeant Billie Gray, Sergeant John C. Matthews, Sergeant First Class Paul N. Scott, Sergeant First Class Melvin C. Taylor and Master Sergeant Clarence G. Oliver, Jr.

Being in the group brought mixed feelings of happiness at going home, along with nostalgia and sadness at leaving friends—many never to be seen again, at least in this world.


The company was again in a reserve location some distance from the front lines, back south toward Yonch'on, as our group prepared to start the first leg of a long trip. Soldiers of the unit were billeted in squad tents. On the morning of our departure, I walked from tent to tent to say "Goodbye" to men in each squad. Invariably, I walked out of each tent with tears welling up in my eyes.

The start of the long trip home would include brief stops in Seoul, Youngdong'po and then to Inch'on for final processing before leaving Korea through the same port where our unit had arrived a few months earlier—but a time period that seemed much longer.

A few days in the replacement depot at Yongdungp'o, under the supervision of the 145th Replacement Company, was a time for receiving new uniforms, resting and trying to impress the very apprehensive new replacements that were arriving and awaiting assignment to combat units.

The departure day finally arrived and the happy troopers loaded on trucks for a short ride to Inch'on in preparation for boarding a ship that would take us on the next leg of the journey home—via a stop in Japan.


The truck convoy dropped all of us off in the Inch'on harbor area and the disorganized horde of soldiers somehow was herded into a large dockside warehouse. This was the site where duffle bags were emptied on the floor so all the contents could be examined to be certain that no weapons, non-personal military items, intoxicating beverages, or other illegal items were mixed among the personal belongings.

For some now long-forgotten reason, I had in my duffle bag a copy of the *United States Code of Military Justice*, a thick hardback bound volume that I had used for reference in my assigned administrative capacity with Company C when some legal reference was needed.

"That is government property," I was advised. "You can't take it home with you," the inspecting officer added as he removed the book and placed it on a growing stack of items that had been removed from other duffle bags. Everything else in my possession seemed to be acceptable for me to keep, my duffle bag was closed and I was pushed on toward the door.

During the two days in the processing center at Inch'on, a few soldiers had acquired bottles of whiskey that they planned to drink during the short trip to Japan. That was not a smart decision.

"Drink it or throw it away," the inspectors advised the owners of the fifths of whiskey, and then adding, "You have an hour before boarding ship."

The partying began.

Several of the happy soldiers had to be helped aboard as the troops loaded onto the flat-bottomed LCU landing craft that was used to shuttle the troops out to the troop transport ship anchored in deeper water outside the shallow Inch'on harbor off the Yellow Sea.

Next stop, Saesbo, Japan.


The trip aboard the ship to Sasebo in the southern part of Japan took about twenty-four hours.

Our arrival in Saesbo was late at night, probably close to midnight. Nothing much could be observed about the harbor or the nearby cities. The ship sailed into India Basin, the harbor area used by large vessels such as the troop ship on which our group had been loaded. After the usual time for the ship's crew to check all moorings, the impatient soldiers finally were routed to the gangway and onto land—another of the Japanese islands.


Although our time in the replacement center in Korea had permitted the opportunity for us to use showers and obtain clean clothes, in truth, the group of soldiers that unloaded on the dock in Sasebo must have been a motley-looking bunch that needed a "good cleaning." A first order of business before we were to be granted much access to this land across the way from Korea was to strip, shower, and get a good "delousing," a powder detoxification to be sure none of us bought any lice to infest Japan.

They were making certain that we were rid of the last vestige of contamination from Korea.

Once again, clean and wearing fresh clothing, our excited and hungry group of nomads was directed into a nearby warehouse-style building that had been converted into a huge dining facility. A freshly prepared meal—with steaks and the trimmings—awaited us.

I remember that we were handed quart bottles of real milk, a true delicacy for us after going months during which only powdered milk was available. The milk supply seemingly was endless, and I know that I drank at least two quarts of milk with the meal, perhaps more.

The memory of the great taste of ice-cold milk remains so strong that I can close my eyes and sense it even now, six decades later.

Sasebo, we learned, was a major port city, located on the northwest coast of the island of Kyushu and with a population of about 250,000 people. With the exception of the Ryukyu Island chain, Kyushu is the southernmost of the Japanese islands. Sasebo was about 600 miles southwest of Tokyo. The southern tip of the Korean peninsula was about 120 nautical miles to the northwest.

A year earlier, those of us in the 45th Infantry Division had been serving as occupation troops on Hokkaido, Japan's northernmost island. Now, here we were on Kyushu at the other end of Japan, on the southernmost major island of the chain of islands that made up that nation.

During our brief stay at the replacement center, I took time to get a little history of the island and the city. Sasebo became an important naval base in 1883 when then Lieutenant Commander Heihachiro Togo nominated the tiny fishing village here to form the nucleus for a base for the Imperial Japanese Navy. In 1904, ships of the Japanese Navy under Admiral Togo sailed from Sasebo to take on the Russian Baltic Fleet. The Imperial Japanese Navy had some 60,000 people working in the dockyard and associated naval station here at the peak of World War II.

When war broke out in Korea, Sasebo became the main launching point for United Nations and the United States forces. Millions of tons of ammunition, fuel, tanks, trucks and supplies flowed through Sasebo on their way to UN Forces in Korea.

Even though our tour of the area was limited to short walks around the extensive camp area, the island appeared to be a beautiful place, with lush foliage. Just off the coast of Sasebo Harbor was the Saikai National Park, a beautiful sea park—an area known as the 99 islands. Sasebo was in the heart of a region renowned for its production of Noritake, Arita, Imari, and Karatsu chinaware. Most of us had purchased some of the famous Japanese china products many months ago while stationed on the island of Hokkaido.

This was an area, though, that had been severely impacted when the United States took its calculated action to use two atomic bombs to force a Japanese surrender to end World War II. Across the bay, just 20 miles south of Saesbo, was the city of Nagasaki—the target of the world's second atomic bomb attack on August 9, 1945.

Only six years and a few months had passed since that attack. Much of Nagasaki was demolished and an estimated 78,000 people, mostly civilians, died from that attack. The Japanese people, especially those who continued to live in this area of Japan in and around the Nagasaki-Saesbo, had not forgotten.

When I looked into the eyes of some of the Japanese people I encountered, one of the questions that ran through my mind was, "What do they really think about us Americans who walk around on their island?" They smiled and seemed friendly. Underneath that façade, though, there must have been some hatred for those who had conquered their land.

I was ready to go home.

In the award-winning movie, *Shenandoah,* James Lee Barrett, the movie scriptwriter, had the primary character in the story reflect on War.

His words were thoughtful and somber.

In the story, Charlie Anderson was a farmer in Shenandoah, Virginia, and found himself—and his family—in the middle of the Civil War. He decided not to get involved in the war because he believed that this was not "his" war. He eventually had to get involved, though, when soldiers in the Union Army took his youngest boy as a prisoner.

Actor James Stewart, who in the movie played the role of farmer Anderson, reflected on war with these words:

> *"There's not much I can tell you about this war. It's like all wars, I guess—The politicians talk about the glory of it. The old men talk about the need of it. And the soldiers, well, they just wanna go home."*[29]

The same feeling applied to our small group from Company C, and the other soldiers fighting in Korea, who "just wanna go home."

The six of us were headed home.

---

[29]Barrett (1965), *Shenandoah*

*The sign on the Saesbo, Japan, dock was a welcome sight. (Below)*
*Master Sergeant J. B. Farnham and Sergeant First Class Paul N.*
*Scott contemplate the days behind and days ahead.*

*Cherry blossoms in the park at the Saesbo Naval Base gave evidence that hope springs eternal, that winter—and War—were behind us, at least for the present. Below, Sergeant First Class Paul N. Scott enjoys visit to park area.*

*(April 1952)*

21 May 1952

Major General James C. Styron
Commanding General
45th Infantry Division
APO 86

Dear General Styron:

In the near future most of the National Guard personnel in the 45th Infantry Division will be leaving the Far East to return home under the Army's phase-out program. Before they leave I want to thank them for a job well done.

I wish to express my admiration for the efficiency and professional competence displayed by these Guardsmen who have been the backbone of the 45th Division. They have accomplished each mission with an enthusiasm and spirit reflecting the high caliber leadership provided by your officers and non-commissioned officers. This must be a source of great pride to you personally.

Please convey to your officers and men the appreciation of myself and my staff for their splendid performance while serving with the Eighth Army in Korea.

My sincere congratulations to the "Thunderbird" Division's National Guardsmen for another "mission accomplished."

Sincerely yours,

t/s JAMES A. VAN FLEET
General, U. S. Army
Commanding

Reproduced by Hq 45
Inf Div, 21 May 52

*General James A. Van Fleet, Commanding General of the Eighth United States Army in Korea, commended soldiers of the 45th Infantry Division for their service in Korea at the time the first of the Oklahoma National Guardsmen were leaving to return to the United States. The letter was "passed on" to units by Major General James C. Styron, the 45th Division commander. General Van Fleet congratulated the "Thunderbird" Division for "another mission accomplished."*

*(Archives, 45th Infantry Division Museum)*

275

# Chapter Twenty

## Home At Last—

The people of Seattle, Washington, were accustomed to seeing soldiers come and go, transported through the city on trucks and buses to and from nearby historic Fort Lawton.

The port of Seattle was a primary port of embarkation and debarkation for troops shipping off to and returning from Korea. Ours was just another shipload of soldiers who were "home from war." There had been thousands before us and thousands more would follow.

That northwestern United States' port is where the *USS Marine Phoenix (T-AP-195)*, the troopship that had been our home at sea for 18 days, docked and returned us to our native land. The sea voyage from Saesbo, Japan, to Seattle had been uneventful. The weather had been good and the sea journey was pleasant.

The trip from Saesbo to Seattle on board the *Marine Phoenix* wasn't exactly a luxury liner ocean cruise, but unexpectedly the Master Sergeant rank I and a few others held resulted in our being provided some very special privileges on board the ship. The old saying, "Rank has its privileges," proved to be true on this occasion.

Most of the soldiers on board the ship were enlisted men. I do not remember seeing any Army officers on the ship and only a small number of the passengers were of Master Sergeant rank, the Army's highest enlisted rank—one considered by the U. S. Navy to be comparable to Chief Petty Officer rank, a very esteemed status in the U.S. Navy and the U.S. Coast Guard branches.

Those of us with that advanced Army rank were placed in Chiefs' quarters—real ship's cabins and real bunks—and ate our meals in the Chief Petty Officer's Mess where excellent meals were served in style. There are many organizations and institutions within the Navy that lay claim to excellence, many that even perform superbly, but the Chief Petty Officer's mess is the most routinely exceptional food service facility on any ship.

The stewards in the Chiefs' Mess on the *Marine Phoenix* certainly held to those standards—at least in my evaluation. We ate and slept in style.

Wow! Living in "Chiefs' quarters" and eating in a "Chiefs' mess" was classy duty for some Infantryman who were not too many days removed from living in bunkers and "chowing down" on Combat rations.

I developed a much greater appreciation for the Navy's Chief Petty Officers, the respect afforded them by both officers and enlisted ranks, and the many privileges awarded to those who achieved that status.

The *Marine Phoenix* was a ship in the Maritime Commission Fleet and briefly had been in the Reserve Fleet after World War II service. Following the invasion of South Korea by North Korean Communists, the *Marine Phoenix* was acquired by the U. S. Navy from the Maritime Commission and assigned to duty with the Military Sea Transportation Service (MSTS).

The ship handled troop lifts to the Far East Command. During the Korean War the ship completed 19 round trips carrying troops and supplies to Japanese and Korean ports including Sasebo, Yokohama, Pusan, and Inch'on.

The *Marine Phoenix* was a ship that could transport more than 2,500 passengers. I don't know the number of soldiers on board on this trip, but learned that there were about 750 returning combat veterans from the 45th Infantry Division on board. Six of us on board were the first soldiers from Company C, 180th Infantry Regiment, to return to the United States after duty in Korea. Also on board were another 15 soldiers from Ada, men who had been serving in other "Thunderbird" units.

As the ship neared the Seattle harbor area, firefighting ships in the bay had their water turrets on full blast, spraying water high into the air, presenting a beautiful "welcome home" water show. Many smaller boats circled the ship as crew members and passengers waved to those of us who lined the deck rails of the troopship.

Emotions were running high. Most of us kept to ourselves those innermost thoughts of happiness about our return and the anxiety in our minds about what might have changed during our months away from home. Most of us silently wondered just how those changes would affect our futures.

Each of us would deal with those concerns later.

Land is land, all over the world, I suppose, but the feeling of returning to the United States after months in a

278

foreign land brought forth emotions that are difficult to describe.

Once off the ship, some of the returning soldiers dropped down and kissed the ground—or, in reality, kissed the dockside pavement. That temptation probably was present in the minds of most of us, but only a few displayed their emotions in that manner.

There was a sense of joy, of being richly blessed, with a great happiness about being back in the United States, and a feeling of prayerful "thanksgiving" for the divine goodness of the safe return.

Seattle wasn't really "home," but this was American land on which we now stood. Home and family were still more than 2,000 miles away and I was eager to start on the last leg of the journey home—a long train ride to Oklahoma.

Perhaps I would "kiss the ground" in Oklahoma when that long journey was completed.


Rows of soldiers quickly moved down the ship's passenger gangway, assembled briefly on the dock and loaded into waiting trucks.

The convoy of trucks drove through some of downtown Seattle and people on the streets and in nearby business buildings waived and cheered as we went along the streets through the business and residential districts on the way to nearby Fort Lawton. The sky was gray, cloudy and threatening rain—standard weather for Seattle.

We were soldiers home from war. Being so enthusiastically greeted by strangers on the streets made us feel very good.


Our next stop—for a few hours—was to be Fort Lawton, a historic military post located on Magnolia Bluff in Seattle, overlooking Puget Sound and nearby Bainbridge Island. Constructed in 1897, Fort Lawton was a busy processing and overseas shipment point during World War II, and when the Korean War began in 1950, the fort served both as an embarkation and debarkation station for thousands of troops headed to and returning from Korea. During the early days of the Korean War, as many as 10,000 replacement troops a day were made ready for transport to Korea at this center.

Somewhat of a history buff, I learned during our brief overnight stay that the fort was originally built to be part of the system of defenses protecting Puget Sound from any naval attack in those early years of the 1900s. The fort was named in honor of Major General Henry Ware Lawton (1843-1899), a veteran of the Civil War and of the Indian Wars, who was killed in action in the Philippines.

The two-story wooden barracks that awaited us at Fort Lawton looked all too familiar to those of us who had been quartered in similar barracks at other forts on other occasions. Nothing fancy here. But, those in charge indicated that this would most likely be a one-night stay. Our transportation to Oklahoma was to be a special troop train that we were scheduled to board the next morning.

During the evening, an attempt was made to make a long distance telephone call to my wife to let her know that our ship had docked, that we were "headed home" and were about to board a train for a trip across the northwest and plains states, eventually to arrive at Fort Sill, Oklahoma.

That "call home" was not to be.

I tried one pay telephone, and another, and another. None of the telephones was operational.

Something was amiss. Soon we learned that telephone operators were "on strike."

That was a real disappointment. I was eager to talk with my wife and had difficulty understanding how something as important as a telephone system would be "shut down" by employees.

No one seemed to have the least bit of concern about our frustration of not being able to call home after returning from overseas duty. The plight of a few soldiers didn't seem to matter.

During the past months, our almost total focus in life was the war. Other than thoughts of family back home, not much of our attention had been given to what was "going on" back in the United States and elsewhere in the world, least of all that of a "strike" that shut down the telephone system.

That disturbed us.

The fact that the war in Korea wasn't on the minds of most people back in the United States was a surprise to us. That reality was brought to our attention with the blunt and somewhat rude remarks of those who responded to our attempted telephone calls with the "we are on strike" comments.

That the lives of a bunch of soldiers just returned from combat were inconvenienced didn't seem to matter a whit.

That was upsetting. It was a harsh return to life "back in the States."

The soldiers just returned from months of combat duty in Korea and eager to contact family back home were an unhappy bunch.

It got worse.

Only a few nighttime hours were spent at the military base outside Seattle. In the pre-dawn darkness, all of us were hustled aboard a Southern Pacific passenger train that would be our traveling home for the next few days for a trip through Washington, Oregon, northern California, then across the mountains and plains to Kansas and eventually south through Oklahoma enroute to Fort Sill, Oklahoma.

The name, "Fort Sill," had a nice sound to it for the trainload of "Okies." That historic military post in southwestern Oklahoma was familiar ground since most of our group had spent some weeks in training at Fort Sill during several summers before the 45th Division was called to active duty at the start of the Korean War.

Soon we would be back in our home state.

For most of us who had little experience with overnight train rides, this trip was a luxury ride. This was a train made up of Pullman sleeper cars and nice dining cars, where courteous crewmembers made life very enjoyable and comfortable. The dining car—complete with nice dining tables and chairs, starched tablecloths, cloth napkins, real silverware and glasses—was a luxury that most of us had not experienced at all, or at least not for a long time. Porters in neat uniforms and waiters in starched and pressed white jackets provided assistance to make the journey comfortable and pleasant.

This was to be an enjoyable ride home.

Shortly after daybreak on the trip south, the train stopped briefly at a station in Oregon, probably as the engineer waited for tracks ahead to be clear. Everyone was told to remain on board during the wait. The car in which I was riding sat immediately adjacent to the station office, and I jumped off the train, ran to the telegraph window with the intent of sending a telegram to my wife to give a report that I was "back in the United States" as well as to give a report on our location and scheduled arrival.

The home front attitude wasn't what I expected.

A station employee very curtly remarked, "Telegraph workers are on strike," for higher wages, working conditions or some such reason that didn't mean much to a bunch of soldiers.

Angry words again were heard up and down the aisles of the passenger cars.

"What a welcome home," one soldier yelled.

That was the point when I realized that for most of the people in the United States, the war in Korea wasn't of much significance in their lives, unless they had family members who were serving in the military. They thought about the war only briefly, if at all, when they listened evening news reports on the radio or spotted a newspaper article that mentioned some battle or gave an update on casualties.

The few families with one of the new television sets watched the evening news as presented by such people as the brusque, cigarette-smoking Edward R. Murrow, the trust-building young Walter Cronkite, or NBC's David Brinkley and Chet Huntley, who later would join together in a tag-team news effort for the historic Huntley-Brinkley Report news analysis program that ran for two decades.

One of the national newscasters, who later would become one of the very visible faces on television in the group known as news "anchors," was a man from our own hometown—Douglas Edwards, who was born in Ada in 1917, the son of two schoolteachers.

Edwards spent his childhood in Ada, but after the death of his father from smallpox in 1930, he and his mother moved to New Mexico. His birth name was Clyde Douglas, but he used the media name of Douglas Edwards and became a household name because of his radio news coverage during World War II, and became the first major newsperson from radio to begin reporting on television in the 1948 era with CBS.

In the spring of 1952, though, the war news was "page two" information as the newscasters on CBS, NBC and ABC gave nightly reports.

*Concern that no one back home would know that soldiers were about to land was an unnecessary fear. The Army notified hometown newspapers of travel plans. The Ada Evening News gave front page space to an article that the first of the 45th Infantry Division soldiers to rotate home were about to land in Seattle.*

# 21 Adans to Land Monday

## Marine Phoenix Due at Seattle with 750 Member: Of 45th Division

SEATTLE, Wash., Apr. 26 (AP) - The Marine Phoenix arrives at Seattle Monday with 750 Oklahoma members of the 45th Division.

Included are the following Scorers:

ADA

Sgt. James E. Roberts
Sgt. Paul N. Scott
Cpl. Jim E. Stone
Sgt. Anvil G. Stout
Sgt. Richard L. Boren
Sgt. James W. Braden
Sgt. Doyle E. Brower
Sgt. Mont G. Comer
Sgt. Billie L. Gray
Sgt. Robert E. Hammond
Sgt. John C. Henry
Sgt. Arthur L. Hester
Sgt. David M. Johnson
Sgt. George E. Jones
Pfc Jessie J. Kyees
Sgt. Donald E. Mathews
Sgt. Roland S. Moore
Sgt. Clarence G. Oliver
Sgt. Jim B. Pamplin
Sgt. Dibrell L. Phillips
Sgt. Pete Phillips

During the days when we were headed home from Korea, on board the *Marine Phoenix* and on the troop train, Murrow, Edwards, Cronkite, Brinkley, Huntley and others spoke of stories such as these:

General Dwight Eisenhower, who had commanded Allied forces to success in World War II fighting in Europe returned to the United States to begin campaigning for the Republican nomination to seek the office of the President of the United States.

President Harry Truman had announced that "under no circumstances" would he run for another term of office as President. Faced with the threat of a massive steel strike involving 600,000 steel workers, President Truman exerted powers recently granted him by the Defense Production Act of 1950 and using his authority as Commander in Chief in time of war, seized the nation's steel mills in order to keep steel production going for the war effort.

Newscasters were still talking about the April 22 first-ever live telecast of an atomic explosion held at the Nevada testing grounds.

And, a tragic collision of two U. S. ships, the aircraft carrier *Wasp* and the destroyer-mine-sweeper *Hobson* was reported. The ships had collided in the Atlantic Ocean, with the loss of 176 lives on the *Hobson*, which sank following the collision.[30]

Perhaps I should not have been so upset about the striking telephone and telegraph workers. The "strike" mood was rather common at the time.

A few weeks later, after I accepted a job as news editor for *The Watonga Republican*, a historic weekly newspaper in the northwestern Oklahoma town of Watonga, I

[30] Linton (1975), p. 376.

learned that 1952 was a peak year for labor union strikes across the nation. News articles about labor union activity reported that at the peak of labor's post-World War II strike wave in 1952 there were 470 major strikes, affecting nearly three million workers nationwide.[31]

Telephone and telegraph workers were just part of that trend.


A newspaper article also reported that a new commander, General Mark W. Clark, would now lead United Nations forces fighting in Korea. He had been named to succeed General Matthew Ridgway, the charismatic leader who had led the forces during our time in Korea,

Interestingly, the major changes in military commanders seemed to occur while we were traveling. The story of General Douglas MacArthur being relieved of command and replaced by General Matthew Ridgway was announced to our troops in April 1951 while we were on board the troopship USNS *General William Weigel* on our way to the Far East command. Now, the man who had replaced General MacArthur and who had been the leader during our time in Japan and Korea, was turning over the command to General Clark, another great general from World War II. That news came to us while we were on a troop train, headed home to Oklahoma.

What a difference a year can make.


The Army must have found a way to send the information about the troop train's scheduled arrival date and time. A report in the *Ada Evening News* advised families of the scheduled arrival.

---

[31] Early (2006)

When the troop train pulled into Fort Sill, hundreds of people were waiting and waving. I was sitting by an open window in the train passenger car, a prime spot that permitted me to lean out the window a bit and scan the sea of faces in search of Vinita.

There she was, holding our son, Paul, with one arm, smiling and waving her free arm. She had spotted me as I leaned out the window.

All of us began jumping from the train steps just as soon as the train slowed to a halt—some of us jumping a bit before authorization was given for a safe exit.


Vinita handed our son, Paul, to one of our parents who was waiting with her and ran toward me as I got off the train. She was looking at me as she ran, and failed to notice a large puddle of muddy water right in her path. She tripped and fell toward the water. Fortunately I was able to catch her before she splashed into the puddle.

Hugs and kisses followed.

With Vinita in my arms, I was really "Home."

*The USS Marine Phoenix (above) brought 750 Oklahomans of the 45ᵗʰ Infantry Division home from Korea in April 1952, unloading the troops at Seattle, Washington. "Thunderbirds" lined the ship's rails (below) to watch as the ship docked after an 18-day trip from Saesbo, Japan.*

# Chapter Twenty One

## After Korea—

As the time for my rotation from Korea to home approached, an invitation was extended for me to accept a direct appointment as a commissioned officer. The offer was very tempting. I loved the military and the prospect of being a commissioned Army officer was very appealing.

I talked at length with some of the officers in Company C and in battalion headquarters, not only seeking counsel and advice, but also to gain a better understanding of what life might be like as an officer instead of a senior noncommissioned officer.

There were some conditions attached to the offer, among them that I would go to Japan for a brief assignment and then return to Korea as an Infantry platoon leader. The offer also included a plan for my wife and son to be able to come to Japan during the assignment there.

The clearly stated intent, though, was that I would soon return to Korea for assignment as an Infantry officer in another company, perhaps even another Army division.

My wife and I "discussed" the matter through a series of airmailed letters to each other. The possibility of pursing a career in the military was seriously considered.

But I longed to see my wife and our son who was born after I deployed overseas.

Ultimately, the decision was made to reject the proposal for a commission, to proceed with the rotation opportunity, to return to Oklahoma, and to be discharged at the end of my term of enlistment.

I have often wondered about what "might have been" if I had chosen to travel that other road.


A few days after arriving home and being reunited with family, my wife and I rented a small garage apartment in Ada for a short time while considering the immediate future and searching for job opportunities. With a wife and child to support, no longer "in the Army" with monthly income, and with only a limited amount of cash on hand, my thoughts were focused on finding a job and preparing for the next phase of our life.

Thoughts about Korea, the war and my friends who were still fighting in that far-off land were pushed to the back of my mind. I was enjoying being reunited with my wife, getting acquainted with our son and beginning the search for job opportunities that I could consider—hopefully in the field of journalism.

That feeling of joy and well-being was short lived. The euphoria bubble was burst when I received an unexpected visit by the parents of one of the soldier friends who were still serving in Korea when I had departed on my journey home.

When I responded to the knock on the front door of our small apartment, I found the parents of Sergeant John R. (Bob) Bush who came to ask if I knew anything about the death of their son. They had just been notified by a telegram from military officials that their son had died. Information about his death was sketchy.

I was unaware of the death until his parents told me of the message they had received. That information was a shock to me. My feelings, though, were nothing compared to the impact that the death notice had on his parents.

The message they received simply advised the parents that their son had been "seriously wounded in action and had died of wounds." They knew nothing of the circumstances. Since I was among the first of area soldiers of the 45th Infantry Division to return to Ada from duty in the Korean War, the parents thought I might be aware of their son's death and the battle or circumstances that resulted in his death.

I learned that Sergeant Bush had died on May 1, just a few days after I had departed from Korea.

I knew nothing of the circumstances surrounding his death.

What could I say to the grieving parents?

Sergeant Bush, although three years younger than I, was an acquaintance from both school days and because of our military service together.

All I could offer were words to let the parents know that their son was a good and brave soldier, and then to offer our condolences to them.

I will never forget the look of deep sorrow on the faces of Mr. and Mrs. Bush as they turned and walked down the wooden steps on the exterior of the garage apartment. This was a time of great sadness—that of parents at the loss of a son and that of a fellow soldier upon learning of the loss of another friend.

Sergeant Bush was just barely 20 years old when he died. He was not to be afforded the opportunity to plan for the future.

For the moment, I felt guilty that I was home, safe, with family and making plans for the future. Such a feeling of guilt is not uncommon among soldiers who survive when others do not live.

A few days later, I applied for and was employed as a newspaper reporter and later news editor for *The Watonga Republican*, one of the state's historic newspapers published in the northwestern Oklahoma city of Watonga—a place I had never visited. My new boss was Gerald (Cowboy) Curtin, one of Oklahoma's greatest and most respected journalists. I was privileged to be working with a master newspaperman.

Then, just a week later, the young Oliver family was living in a land of "waiving wheat," meeting wonderful new friends and learning about another community.

Life was good!

# Epilogue—

Shortly after our return to the United States and our move to Watonga, in northwestern Oklahoma, federal and state leaders began an effort to organize a parallel 45$^{th}$ Infantry Division (NG) in Oklahoma in anticipation of the eventual end of the Korean War, the deactivation of the division, and the return of the division and its "colors" from Korea to Oklahoma.

The search was on for new officers to help organize the scores of hometown units that were being planned across the state, matching the historic "Thunderbird" units.

The door to becoming a commissioned officer began to swing open—once again. Although I had declined the invitation to become a commissioned officer during my last few days in Korea, I still had a great love for the military, wanted to be involved in the newly organized unit, and reconsidered the idea of becoming an officer.

I applied for a direct appointment from noncommissioned ranks to commissioned officer status, and was commissioned a Second Lieutenant, Infantry, in a brief ceremony at the historic 45$^{th}$ Division Headquarters Armory in Oklahoma City.

Thus began a new chapter of my life.

Although I was to enjoy some success in careers in both journalism and education, a patriotic military thread was to continue running through the fabric of my life.

Upon receiving the new appointment, I became a platoon leader and later executive officer of Company L, 179th Infantry Regiment, in the newly organized stateside 45th Infantry Division (NG) while the active duty Division remained in Korea.

In August 1953, after deciding to return to college to complete studies that had been interrupted by war, I moved my young family back to Ada where I enrolled in East Central State College (the present East Central University).

In the months that followed, a transfer of military assignment was completed and I was named commanding officer of Headquarters Company, First Battalion, 180th Infantry Regiment, and served in that capacity until I accepted a job in Broken Arrow in August 1955. That relocation caused a transfer to Company E, 279th Infantry Regiment, where I served first as executive officer and later as company commander.

Following completion of the Infantry Company Officers Course at the Infantry School at Fort Benning, Georgia, in 1958-1959, I was promoted to Captain, and later transferred to a staff assignment with Second Battalion, 279th Infantry, serving as the battalion S-2.

My military career was on a "fast track" and I soon was assigned to the 45th Division Brigade S-2 post in 1964 and promoted to Major, Infantry, serving on General David Matthews's Brigade staff, with plans for another assignment and another promotion pending.

The dream of having continued leadership opportunities and other promotions disappeared suddenly in May 1965 when I was felled with a serious heart attack that almost took my life, and certainly resulted in a drastic change in my life.

Some friends and family members had cautioned that I was "burning the candle at both ends" with my full-time work in school administration, attending the University of Tulsa graduate school in studies toward a doctor's degree, serving in a challenging military assignment that required frequent travel throughout a vast area of the state and handling a variety of civic, community and church responsibilities.

They were correct in that assessment. My life plans were altered.

One distinguished cardiologist advised me to "quit work" and "go play golf." When I asked about my life expectancy, another cardiologist indicated that I might live to see our daughter "graduate from high school." That meant living to perhaps 40 years of age.

Those words were disheartening. I had a wife and three children to support. I could not "go play golf," even if I knew how to play that game, and I certainly did not intend to die at age 40, as one doctor speculated might occur.

After several weeks of hospitalization and rehabilitation following the heart attack, I returned to work in a part-time capacity and eventually was able to resume my work on a fulltime basis.

My military service plans, though, were derailed.

I was transferred to inactive status for a period of time, and then transferred to the U. S. Army Reserve School to continue service and study in the Advanced Infantry Officers Course, including additional service at the Infantry School in Fort Benning, Georgia, to complete the Advanced Infantry Officers Course.

My assignment in the USAR Control Group continued until September 1970. I had been given a Mobilization Designation calling for an assignment to Fort Riley, Kansas, possibly to lead a training battalion in the event of my ever being needed for active service.

Later, my assignment was changed to that of being a psychological operations officer at the John F. Kennedy Center for Special Military Assistance at Fort Bragg, North Carolina, attached to the Special Forces 1st Psychological Operations Battalion.

That Special Forces assignment proved to be tremendously interesting and challenging. While on duty at Fort Bragg, I asked the battalion commander, a Colonel, a graduate of the United States Military Academy at West Point, with Airborne, Ranger and Special Forces qualifications, and obviously on the "fast track" for flag status and Army leadership assignments, about my unexpected assignment to the Psychological Operations unit.

That was an elite unit in which every member was a college graduate, many with advanced degrees, in which all unit members were fluent in at least two languages, and all were "jump qualified" Special Forces soldiers.

The learned battalion commander held several advanced degrees, including one in doctorial studies. He was the son of a West Point graduate who was a retired general, and his grandfather also was a West Point graduate and a general. Obviously, this commander was among the Army's finest leaders.

I reminded him that, although I was nearing completion of a doctorial degree in leadership studies and research, that I had only limited knowledge of another language and, that even though I had studied some psychology, was not an expert in that educational discipline. In addition, I was a "straight-leg" Infantryman who had never "jumped out of an airplane" for any reason—certainly not for Airborne qualification.

Although my previous battalion and brigade staff assignments had been as a military intelligence officer, I had to ask him, "How did the Army in all it's infinite wisdom pull my name out of the massive computer system containing all the personnel records and assign me to Fort Bragg, North Carolina, for service in a Psychological Operations Battalion?"

The commander chuckled, and then advised me that I had been selected because of my undergraduate studies in journalism. Presumably, because of that background, I could be considered qualified to assist in writing and developing propaganda materials that could be used in the print media and radio broadcast psychological operations mission of the unit.

I was greatly impressed with that commander and all members of his very elite Army unit. Being associated with the unit was an honor, and I was pleased to hold that Mobilization Designation assignment for a few years.

As my age and years of service continued to mount, the countdown began to bring an end to my military career I transferred to a Retired Reserve status in 1986 and to Retired status in July 1989—42 years after my first enlistment in 1947 as a 17-year-old private in Company C, 180th Infantry Regiment.

Interestingly, my service with Company C, 180th Infantry Regiment and the later choice of Broken Arrow, Oklahoma, as my "adopted home town" created a unique link with one of my personal heroes, Lieutenant Colonel Ernest Childers.

Because of the unusual connection of having military service in the same unit—but in different wars—and our mutual "hometown" status, Colonel Childers and I became friends.

We also became bonded even more when we two long-time "Thunderbirds" who served in the same infantry company a decade apart and in two different wars—one during World War II and one during the Korean War—

were paid tribute by the Broken Arrow community by having schools named in our honor.

A newspaper article about the naming of the schools pointed out: "Lieutenant Colonel Ernest Childers, a Medal of Honor recipient and hometown Broken Arrow war hero, and Major Clarence G. Oliver, Jr., Ed.D., recognized as an educator, journalist, soldier and civic leader in the community for 50 years, were honored when new middle schools were named in their honor."[32]

The Broken Arrow's Board of Education granted exceptions to a long-standing policy of not naming schools in honor of living individuals with the naming of Ernest Childers Middle School, dedicated in 1985, and the Clarence G. Oliver, Jr., Middle School in 1995.

Although our paths were crossed, our backgrounds were different—except for Company C, the 180th Infantry Regiment, and our mutual ties with a special hometown, Broken Arrow, Oklahoma.

In 1940, Childers, a Creek-Cherokee Indian, was a student in the Chilocco Indian School in northern Oklahoma. Male students at the school were known as cadets and they had military classes as part of the regular curriculum.

They also had their own National Guard unit—Company C, 180th Infantry—that was made up entirely of Indians. The unit was activated in 1940, and that active status was extended in 1941 when the United States entered World War II.

Childers, along with most of his male classmates, went on active duty. He first wore the distinctive "Thunderbird" insignia of Oklahoma's famed 45th Division at

---

[32] "Broken Arrow Middle Schools Named for Two 'Thunderbirds'," *45th Division News*, February 2004.

Fort Sill during basic training. It was an emblem he would honor throughout a long and distinguished military career.

Colonel Childers retired from active duty in 1965 after almost 30 years military service. Following his retirement, he returned to his hometown area and lived in the neighboring city of Coweta until his death in 2005.


I was a Broken Arrow school administrator for 30 years and superintendent of schools when the Childers school was constructed. Because of Colonel Childers' national hero status, I urged the board of education to name the new school in his honor in 1985.

I first learned of Childers' heroic action while studying the history of Company C, 180th Infantry Regiment, when I enlisted in that unit while still a 17-year-old high school senior in Ada and learned about the young Second Lieutenant who became a national hero.

We two became personally acquainted while I was serving as a "Thunderbird," commanding Company E, 279th Infantry Regiment, in Childers' hometown. Colonel Childers was on active duty at the time.

The friendship of two "Thunderbirds" lasted 50 years—until his death in 2005.


Our friendship became a closer relationship during the late 1970s when Colonel Childers wanted the Medal of Honor Society to hold its annual convention in his hometown. This and some later contacts permitted me to expand that friendship to include members of his wonderful family—his lovely wife, Yolanda, and their children, Elaine, Donna and Ernie.

In those days, Broken Arrow didn't have hotel facilities that could be a home base for such an event, so nearby

Tulsa facilities had to be used in that support role. But, to Ernest Childers, the convention was "in Broken Arrow."

I was honored to be asked to serve as a co-chairman of the Medal of Honor Society's events in Broken Arrow, and thus was privileged to work closely with Colonel Childers and some of his associates with the planning and during the activities.

Colonel Childers insisted that many of the events to be in his hometown, and through his leadership, Broken Arrow was chosen to host the group with a downtown parade like no other this community has ever seen, followed by a luncheon to honor the society members, their families, and special guests.

That turned out to be a fantastic time for Broken Arrow.

Watching more than 150 Medal of Honor recipients in a parade along Broken Arrow's Main Street, some marching in a group, others riding in cars and a special bus, was a thrill for the thousands who lined Main Street, cheering, waving flags, applauding, saluting and crying.

Few communities have experienced such a parade involving so many national heroes.

The lump in my throat, caused by being in the presence of that many of our nation's greatest heroes, seemed to remain for weeks. Even now, three decades after the event, I still get "goose bumps" just thinking of the occasion.


When the Broken Arrow Board of Education agreed on the name for the community's next middle school in 1995, I had been retired from the school system for three years and was serving as Dean of the Oral Roberts University School of Education. Although the school leaders were aware of the military service of both of us, only Colonel Childers and I were aware that both of us had served in Company C, 180th Infantry Regiment.

The unit bond was treasured.

Photographs and artifacts of the years of "Thunderbird" service of both of us can be found in display cases in the museum rooms of the two schools.

Both of us had the opportunity to be regular visitors at the two middle schools, serving as guest speakers for classes, assembly programs, Veterans Day and other patriotic events, and to sign hundreds of school yearbooks for students each spring.

Both the middle schools were designed with museum space adjacent to the front lobbies. The rooms are filled with photographs, books, medals, flags, and artifacts to recognize the military and civic service of the two honorees. In addition, the school mascots are the "Thunderbirds" for Childers Middle School and the "Eagles" for Oliver Middle School.

Interestingly, the new middle schools that recognized two former "Thunderbirds" were designed by the architectural firm of Coleman and Schneider, with one of the primary architects being Kinney E. Coleman, once Sergeant First Class Coleman of the 180th Infantry Regiment's Service Company, and the personnel sergeant whose friendship with me began in 1950 and who made possible the "Restful Night in Yongdungp'o" that is told in one of the stories in this book.

The Broken Arrow community commissioned and erected an impressive bronze statue of Colonel Childers, created by internationally known Indian sculptor Allan Houser. The statue is located in Veterans' Park on Main Street, Broken Arrow.

Oral Roberts University President Richard Roberts and his wife Lindsey commissioned a bronze bust of me, then serving as the Dean of the ORU School of Education.

The bust, created by artist Brenda Angel Copeland, is in the lobby of Oliver Middle School.

Lieutenant Colonel Childers died in 2005. I was privileged to be among those asked by his family to speak at the memorial service held to honor this great hero. Appropriately, the service was held in Childers Middle School.

Here are some of the words I spoke that day:

*"Special destinies cause our paths to cross, impacting our lives in unique ways. Often, that crossing of paths creates wonderful friendships. That is how I feel about my friendship with Ernest Childers. Ernest Childers is of the special group that has come to be known as The Greatest Generation."*

Not only was Ernest Childers of the much-discussed "Greatest Generation," he also was part of an even more special group, the Medal of Honor recipients. There is an unusual bond of brotherhood and comradeship among all living recipients of the Medal of Honor. No amount of money, power or influence can buy one's rite of passage to this exclusive circle of heroes.

Even though he was one of our nation's greatest military heroes, Ernest Childers was a kind, gracious and humble man. Of his heroic action that earned the nation's highest medal for valor, he would often quote the nineteenth century American writer Ralph Waldo Emerson who once wrote, *"A hero is no braver than an ordinary man, but he is braver five minutes longer."*

Ernest Childers had a great vision for this nation—and a concern for its future.

That concern was made clear to me one day during a conversation with him when he was making one of his many visits to speak with students at Childers Middle School. He spoke about the uneasy era in which we live, and expressed concern that young people should be taught that we must not be tempted to abandon the time-honored principles that have been established and confirmed by previous generations.

He shared the feeling that our American values are not luxuries, but necessities and must be preserved—that they are not the salt in our bread, but the very bread itself.

About all a man can hope for in life is to set an example for others and, when he is gone, to be an inspiration to others.

Ernest Childers did that in a remarkable way.

During the time of preparation for the memorial service to honor Colonel Childers, I learned from Mrs. Childers that Ernest's favorite religious hymn was the inspirational song, *Onward, Christian Soldiers.*

When that hymn is sung, one can visualize a parade of people—perhaps many in uniform just like Colonel Childers—singing loudly and marching with banners held high.

The first stanza of that wonderful hymn includes these words:

*"Like a mighty army moves the Church of God;*
*Brothers, we are treading where the saints have trod.*
*We are not divided, all one body we-*
*One in hope and doctrine, one in charity. "*[33]

It is very appropriate for a hero of his stature to have embraced such an impressive Christian marching hymn.

The words speak to Colonel Ernest Childers' commitment and his faith. I believe he would recommend to all of us—family, friends, students, colleagues and most certainly his fellow soldiers—the message of that hymn.

---

[33]Barkley (1979), p.174.

Although overshadowed by World War II, which was barely over before the conflict in Korea erupted, the Korean War was a bitter war fought in a distant land. The war began on June 25, 1950, when the North Korean Army launched an invasion into South Korea. Before a controversial armistice ground the war to a halt July 27, 1953, soldiers from the United States and 21 other U.N. countries battled the North Korean and Chinese armies up and down the Korean peninsula.

The United States suffered 140,000 killed, wounded or imprisoned in the Korean War.

An Armistice was reached on July 27, 1953.

Korea remained a divided land.

Most of us who participated in that war to stop the spread of Communism are proud of being a part of that idealistic effort.

Mission accomplished!

*Master Sergeant Clarence G. Oliver, Jr., in Japan prior to the deployment of the 45th Infantry Division to Korea.*

*(Summer, 1951)*

*Clarence G. Oliver, Jr., received a direct appointment as a Second Lieutenant, Infantry, in 1952 and served in assignments with the 179th Infantry Regiment, the 180th Infantry Regiment, the 279th Infantry Regiment, and as a 45th Division Brigade staff officer. Oliver is pictured here in 1956 as a First Lieutenant and newly appointed Company Commander of Company E, 279th Infantry Regiment, based in Broken Arrow, Oklahoma.*

## Acknowledgments—

There are so many people who have provided encouragement and assistance to me during the days of research and writing of this book that I most certainly will overlook someone and fail to give proper acknowledgment to all who deserve my words of appreciation.

For any such unintentional oversight, I sincerely apologize.

I gratefully acknowledge these special people:

My wife, Vinita, who has been the love of my life since she was 15 years old, deserves a big hug for her patience with me and for her kind understanding of the time commitment—the days, late evenings and week ends—that were required to research and write this book.

Our daughter, Shirley J. Parsons, sons, Paul A. Oliver and Mark G. Oliver, and their spouses, as they read bits and pieces of draft chapters, showed interest in the writings and gave encouraging words to continue the telling of the story.

Brigadier General Gerald Wright, former Air Force jet fighter pilot, retired commander of the Oklahoma Air National Guard, retired Oklahoma State Senator, and long-time friend, provided almost weekly encouragement and persistently "urged" me to tell the "rest of the story."

Extraordinary appreciation is extended to some of the finest soldiers in the world from Company C, 180th Infantry Regiment, with whom we shared experiences in the United States, Japan and during the days in Korea. They provided stories, photographs, offered suggestions, helped with research activities, assisted with identification of others in photographs, and shared their own memories of those days.

Thus, I say a singular "Thank You" to these old soldiers from Company C—Harold Gene Evans of Ada, Oklahoma, Master Sergeant and former First Sergeant; Paul N. Scott of Ada, Oklahoma, Sergeant First Class and unit supply sergeant; Dr. Joe Mac Floyd of Cookeville, Tennessee, Sergeant, squad leader, and later an Emeritus Professor at Tennessee Technology University, Cookeville, Tennessee, whose personal account of a wounded soldier's rescue and recovery is a major part of this book.

Kemper W. Chambers of Morristown, New Jersey, Corporal in Company C's second platoon, provided unusual assistance in helping "track down" newspaper information and photographs in Newark, New Jersey, and in providing essential facts related to those long-ago days in Korea. He did so even while busy at work completing his own new book, *A Walk Into the Past.*

Praises go to Joe Hill Floyd of Hobbs, New Mexico, Sergeant First Class, a squad leader, and his wife, Glynese, for their many hours of research, consultation and for sharing artifacts and photographs to help enhance the story. Sergeant Hill and his long-time friend, Dr. James A. West of Edmond, Oklahoma, Sergeant First Class, an assistant platoon sergeant, and later University Professor, are two

307

men whose heroic actions are recorded in this book and whose lives had great impact on many others. Unfortunately, their untimely deaths prevent their having the opportunity to read about their story.

Appreciation for the support offered by museum curators is extended to Denise Neil-Binion, former assistant curator of the 45th Infantry Division Museum, Oklahoma City, and later the senior curator of the World War II Victory Museum in Auburn, Indiana; and to Michael E. Gonzales, curator of the 45th Infantry Division Museum and a Major with the modern-day "Thunderbirds" that still make Oklahomans proud. These two specialists opened the doors of the museum archives and helped me search through stacks of boxes and many file cabinets for historical records, artifacts, maps and photographs. I am grateful. Kevin O'Sullivan of the Associated Press Images in New York City deserves my gratitude for his effort in delving deep into the Associated Press archives of old negatives to find a 1951 photograph that very vividly tells the story of a dramatic mountain rescue of a wounded soldier. He could have said the search task was too challenging, but he was intrigued with the request and persevered.

Two highly successful authors of award-winning books of soldiers in another war were very gracious with their words of encouragement and their assistance in guiding me to the right source for a very meaningful quotation to set the tone for why this book was written.

Joseph L. Galloway, journalist, Vietnam War veteran, war correspondent, is the Military Affairs Editor for Knight Ridder Newspapers and co-author of the book, *We Were Soldiers Once and Young*. He offered encouragement and pointed me in the right direction to find the "right source."

That source proved to be Michael Norman, author of the captivating book, *These Good Men: Friendships Forged in War*, and now a Professor in the College of Arts and Sciences of New York University. This one-time Sergeant in

308

the U. S. Marine Corps during the Vietnam War and eloquent wordsmith composed the haunting words of the treatise, "Such Good Men," and granted permission for those words to be used to introduce this book to help explain why there is such a unique bond among men who have served together in combat. I am grateful for his encouragement and support.

Friends who are willing to offer constructive critique of another's writing effort are held in particular esteem. Billie Jean (Fathree) Floyd, a friend of many decades, even from high school days, a former Oklahoma State Senator and a Professor at East Central University in Ada, Oklahoma, reviewed and critiqued draft chapters from an unusual perspective. Some of the words are about her late husband, Ben C. Floyd, Sergeant First Class, and his younger brother, Joe Mac Floyd, both prominent in stories contained in this book. Some of her comments and suggestions came with tears. She is a treasured friend.

Another such trusted colleague, Dr. Sherri D. Tapp, President of *Tapp Into Excellence!*, motivational speaker, consultant and Associate Professor of Graduate Education at Oral Roberts University, offered important observations and suggestions. Her analysis of content, theme and "teaching moments" has been helpful and is greatly respected.

I am indebted to Adam J. Foreman of Broken Arrow, Oklahoma, one of the most talented of graphic artists, for his valuable aid in transforming my draft ideas into such an impressive and inviting book cover. He is noted for his volunteerism and his *Pro bono publico* efforts in promoting many Broken Arrow community groups, especially for his work with the Broken Arrow Arts and Humanities Council. I am grateful for his assistance.

For all the others who inquired about "when?" and expressed encouraging words through the many months when this has been "a work in progress," I also express my appreciation.

All of you are wonderful, gracious friends. I struggle with how to express appreciation for all the support. The two small words, "Thank You," seem so inadequate; but, until I can find better words, these are written to each of you with sincere gratitude.

Clarence G. Oliver, Jr.
Broken Arrow, Oklahoma
2007

# —References—

Ambrose, Stephen E., *Band of Brothers: E Company, 506th Regiment, 101st Airborne from Normandy to Hitler's Eagle's Nest*, (1992), Simon and Schuster, New York, New York.

Ambrose, Stephen E., *D-Day, June 6, 1944: The Climactic Battle of World War II* (1994), Simon and Schuster, New York, New York.

Barkley, John M., editor. *Handbook to the Church Hymnary*, *3rd edition* (1979), Oxford University Press, London, England.

Barrett, James Lee. *Shenandoah*, (1965), screenplay directed by Andrew V. McLaglen, Universal Pictures Company, Inc., Hollywood, California.

Cash, Fannie C. *God's Message: A Book of 365 Daily Meditations*, *(1948)*, Universal Book and Bible House, Philadelphia, Pennsylvania.

Churchill, Sir Winston S. *The Story of the Malakand Field Force*, (1898). Longmans, Green & Company, London, England.

Cole, Paul M. *The Korean War. POW/MIA Issues: Volume 1, Report No. MR-351/1-USDP* (1994). National Defense Research Institute, The Rand Corporation, Santa Monica, California.

Early, Steve. "Is The Strike Dead? Not According to Bob Schwartz," MRZine. January 3, 2006. <http://www.zmag.org/contnt/showarticle.cfm?SectionID=15ItemID=9452>.

Ginder, P.D. Memorandum (undated). Headquarters, 45th Infantry Division, APO 45, Office of the Commanding General. Archives, 45th Infantry Division Museum, Oklahoma City, Oklahoma.

Goulden, Joseph C. *Korea, The Untold Story of the War* (1982). Times Books, division of Quadrangle/The New York Times Book Company, Inc., New York, New York.

Hourihan, William J. *A Brief History of the United States Chaplain Corps.* United States Army Chaplain Center and School, Fort Jackson, South Carolina. <http://www.usachcs.army.mil/history/chapter_7.htm>.

Linton, Calvin D. *The Bicentennial Almanac: 200 Years of America*, (1975). Thomas Nelson, Inc., New York, New York.

Marshall, S.L.A. *Commentary on Infantry Operations and Weapons Usage in Korea, Winter of 1950-51.* (1953), Operations Research Office, The Johns Hopkins University, Chevy Chase, Maryland

Michael Norman, Michael, *These Good Men: Friendships Forged from War,* (1989). Crown Publishers, Inc., New York, New York.

Ridgway, General Matthew B., Memorandum, Subject: "Why We Are Here," (January 21, 1951). Headquarters Eighth U.S. Army (EUSAK), Office of the Commanding General.

*The Holy Bible: New International Version* (1973, 1978,1984). International Bible Society, The Zondervan Corporation, Grand Rapids, Michigan.

*The Author—*

Clarence G. Oliver, Jr., served as a Master Sergeant in an Infantry Rifle Company during the Second Winter Campaign of the War in Korea.

An award-winning journalist, a former United States Army Infantry officer and a retired Superintendent of Schools, he also is Emeritus Dean and Professor at Oral Roberts University.

He and his wife, Vinita, married 57 years, have three children, seven grandchildren and a great-grandson.

The Olivers live in historic Broken Arrow, Oklahoma.

Printed in the United States
97854LV00005B/1-90/A